10 2020

D0978748

Still Sideways

Riding the
Edge Again After
Losing My Sight

DEVON RANEY

patagonia

DISCARD

PACIFIC GROVE PUBLIC LIBRARY
550 CENTRAL AVENUE
PACIFIC GROVE, CA 93950
(831) 648-5760

796.939092
RANEY

Still Sideways
Riding the Edge Again After Losing My Sight

Patagonia publishes a select list of titles on wilderness, wildlife, and outdoor sports that inspire and restore a connection to the natural world.

Copyright 2019 Devon Raney
Foreword © Tom Burt, Jeff Hawe
Photograph copyrights held by the photographer as indicated in captions.

All rights reserved. No part of this book may be used or reproduced in any manner whatsoever without written permission from the publisher and copyright holders. Requests should be emailed to books@patagonia.com or mailed to Patagonia Books, Patagonia Inc., 259 W. Santa Clara St., Ventura, CA 93001-2717.

Hardcover Edition

Printed in Canada on 100 percent post-consumer recycled paper.

Editors – Sarah Morgans, John Dutton
Photo Editor – Kyle Sparks
Designer/Art Director – Christina Speed
Project Manager – Jennifer Patrick
Production – Rafael Dunn
Photo Production – Sus Corez
Creative Director – Bill Boland
Creative Advisor – Jennifer Ridgeway
Director of Books – Karla Olson

Hardcover ISBN 978-1-938340-89-5
E-Book ISBN 978-1-938340-90-1
Library of Congress Control Number 9781938340895

Published by Patagonia Works

Front cover: Devon Raney nailing a turn in the 2012 Dirksen Derby. Mount Bachelor, Oregon. *Jeff Hawe*

Front endpaper: Sensing a tube and hoping to find it. Mexico. 2018. *Colin Wiseman*

First spread: Tom Herron and I stop for a wave check in October during a 100-year storm—I'm not seeing much, but I'm certainly hearing the rumble. Oregon. 2013. *Jeff Hawe*

Pages 2–3: Following Tom Burt down the course at the 30th annual Mount Baker Legendary Banked Slalom. Washington. 2016. *Kevin McHugh*

Page 4: Devon Raney, 2013. *Jeff Hawe*

Contents

Forewords

Tom Burt, World-Renowned Pro Snowboard Rider and Designer
Jeff Hawe, Adventure Sports Photographer

Tom Burt: Make a fist with each hand and put them right up close to your eyes—almost touching your eyes, with your thumbs touching your nose. This is what I imagine Devon can see from his description of his vision. Try it before you read any more, just to get an idea.

Devon obviously doesn't see much. His central vision is gone. Just his peripheral vision is left. This means his brain only catches contrast and motion, but only out to about twenty feet away. His only vision in focus is within about six inches of his eyes. An example: when he crosses the street, he doesn't know where to step off the curb because there is no contrast to the street, everything looks flat, but as he walks to the other side, the vertical of the curb creates contrast due to the shadows and he knows something is there and steps up it.

He uses his eyes differently than you or me by moving his eyes up, down, or sideways to move his peripheral vision where he wants to look. If he is following me snowboarding, he never looks at me directly, but moves his eyes so his peripheral vision catches my contrast and motion. He then just has to trust me and follow. But we still have to be in that twenty-foot range. He can read

Opposite: Nose to the grindstone. I have to supersize the type on the computer screen to write. 2016. *Jeff Hawe*

off a computer but he has to sit within that half foot of a large screen and blow up the image to read only a couple words at a time across the screen. Emails are manageable, but a book would take painstakingly long to read, so audiobooks are now his staple. If you meet Devon, you might not even be aware that he can't see you. He doesn't use a cane. He will walk into the room, shake your hand, and walk around the room without running into anything. Most people are fooled by this charade and it puts him at a disadvantage. The water is the most comfortable place with his vision loss because a wave has contrast and motion as it stands up and breaks. He surfs amazingly well by reading that motion and contrast of the wave to dip under the lip for a quick cover up, hit the lip, or cut back, usually riding the wave to its end. Most people in the water have no clue that they are invisible to him. But since he can't see if someone else is on that wave when he takes off, he sometimes drops in on another surfer; a no-no in surf etiquette, so people can get pissed at him. If I'm in the water, it is easy for me to defuse a pissed-off surfer by explaining Devon's vision, but he is often surfing by himself, and doesn't say a word. Instead, he leaves the water, not wanting to cause more of a scene.

Devon has a try-it-and-see-what-works attitude that lets him get away with this style of approach. He is not afraid to go for it, but at the same time, he pays the price when something goes wrong. It can be mental, like dropping in on someone, but it is usually a physical price, like when he is following me snowboarding and the snow changes from flat to bumpy. He of course cannot see it and gets tossed. He takes brutal falls, but Devon always gets back up, tries to shake it off, and keeps going, even when he is obviously in pain.

He rarely gets discouraged, but sometimes all the challenges get him mentally beat down, frustrated, and discouraged by not being able to accomplish something because he can't see. That is where it is important to consider what he wants to do and that it may have to be done in a different way. Whenever I'm around and I see the frustration, I put my fist to my eyes, imagine what he can see, and try to figure out how we can come up with a way to get it done. We have overcome a few things together, but he is the one who really has to deal with his life's new challenges. And in most ways he has. He has swallowed his pride over not being able to provide for his family, being dependent upon others, and accepting that certain things he just cannot do anymore. He now needs help for many things that are no-brainers for a sighted person. At the same time he is always reinventing new ways for himself to lessen those burdens by trying new ways of doing things and thus be more independent.

His wife, Rebecca, and daughter, Madrona, have been amazing. Those two have had to take the brunt of the changes to their lives head-on and help Devon navigate his new path. That path has led to him writing this book and opening up his life, thoughts, heart, and soul. Writing is something he can do well with or without vision.

Beyond the challenges that Devon has had to overcome— maybe because of those challenges—the part of Devon that distinguishes him is his mind and approach to life. Devon will drop it all to watch the sunset, though I am not so sure what he can see of it. (Maybe it is more of a feeling?) He will go surfing, snowboarding, get a pastry, cheer his daughter on, or take a walk with Becca. He will light a fire, have a coffee with honey and cream, make someone laugh, joke about things that suck for the blind— like sandwich boards on sidewalks—build something, anything, himself. The list goes on. He acts like he doesn't think himself limited in any way, the only limit being how to figure out a way to do something.

Devon inspires me to keep figuring things out even though it may seem impossible, laugh and joke at things that suck, keep doing the things I love, and enjoy my family and friends. I count myself lucky to call Devon my friend, someone I can learn from, laugh with, ride with, try to learn new ways of doing things with, and most of all, be inspired by. My hope is that you too will laugh, learn, and be inspired by Devon through his writing. Enjoy.

———

Jeff Hawe: In February of 2012 I knew who he was—vaguely at least. The blind snowboarder I'd seen following Tom Burt down the Baker Banked Slalom course. *Rad guy,* I thought. It was cool to see somebody not letting a disability stop him from enjoying his passions. At that time, my understanding of Devon Raney and the things I would learn from him went no deeper.

Later that year, in December, I got a call that in certain ways changed my life. Not immediately, but it sparked a friendship that would. I received an assignment to take photographs of Devon snowboarding. There was a race coming up at Mount Bachelor, Oregon, the Dirksen Derby, in which Devon would be competing. Coordinating with Colin Wiseman, the editor of *The Snowboarder's Journal*, I met up with him and Devon early on race day. We talked and made some plans, then Devon started warming up on the course, following Colin closely through hairpin-tight banked turns snaking down the course. He rode with skill.

Later that day, after we had captured enough images for the story, Colin retired to the lodge for an après beer and I left my camera backpack with him, opting to go ride fast laps with Devon. I was intrigued by this guy. After he taught me the simple system for being his riding point man, we picked a few favorite runs and rode them until the chair closed for the day. He astonished me. I was riding fast through wide-open runs, down into tight winding gullies, and through the trees. Every time I would glance back over my shoulder to see where Devon was, he was right on my tail, pushing me faster. *Dude rips!* I thought to myself.

Yet it was more than his riding that captivated me. It was the stories he told on the lift rides back to the top. He is an inspiring person, and that has nothing to do with his lack of vision. We parted Mount Bachelor promising to meet up again that winter. Unfortunately, my busy season schedule got in the way.

It wasn't until mid-May that we finally linked up again; Colin and I joined Devon on the Washington coast for a weekend surf trip. It was a cold and rainy weekend with junk waves, so we passed most of the time drinking hot coffee and trading stories in his yellow camper in between intermittent soggy surf checks. That weekend Devon told me about his plans for a coastal surf trip, Washington to Mexico, via bicycle. It sounded like an incredible adventure. He had a dialed-in plan. Different friends would fly in and meet him along the journey to captain his tandem for a weeklong leg each. Devon would be the only rider on the entirety of the trip. A bike, a couple saddlebags full of food, clothing, and camping gear, and a trailer with wetsuits and surfboards. The mission sounded minimal and dedicated, and it piqued my interest.

He called a few weeks after that weekend to ask advice on what kind of camera to purchase for the trip. I casually suggested he take a photographer instead, and I knew just the guy. He paused, seemingly giving it some quick thought, then said yeah, I should come along. I would be on my own bike, accompanying the tandem. As we talked and made plans, Devon's excitement grew and I felt a great sense of inclusion. I found myself just waiting for the summer to pass so we could start pedaling in September.

Fast-forward to late September, roughly two weeks into the trip in coastal Oregon. It had been raining as if Noah had just finished building an ark somewhere. Every day we were soaked, cold, and tired. My knees were having issues with the continuous fifty-to-sixty-mile days. Several large storms had whipped the ocean into a massive churning mess. There was no surfing, just riding in the rain. It was not what I had in my mind's eye for this trip. My morale was low. The captain of the tandem on this stretch was a fit cyclist named Tom Herron. Between him, Devon, and the advantages of a tandem I could not keep up, so I was riding alone and way behind.

Devon is notoriously not a patient person, so I know that the amount of time he had to wait for me to catch up was not easy for him. Yet every time I would pull into whatever spot they had stopped at, Devon would greet me excitedly, full of upbeat positivity. If he was frustrated with waiting for me, he never let it show.

As the trip progressed, the weather improved, the waves cleaned up, the sun came out, and my body acclimated. We began to fulfill what we'd set out to do: ride and surf every day. We stopped in at local schools to give talks to kids about pursuing passions and dreams in life. We made new friends everywhere we went. Many people, just hearing what we were doing, would offer us a place to stay, have us over for a meal, or share something cool from their lives. It had become the incredible journey we'd envisioned.

Needless to say, I got to know Devon quite well along the way. I annoyed him with my thorough and methodical—slow—approach to our daily routine of wake, caffeinate, eat, pedal, surf, pedal, eat, sleep, repeat. He got under my skin with his go, go, go approach. This subtle tension became fodder for making jokes on behalf of each other and laughing it off.

I realized that with Devon, there is an innate, bordering on manic, desire to keep going and doing. When the rest of the crew would be happy to stop and take in a view, Devon would wait, writhing silently, to get the wheels turning again. What fun is pausing to enjoy your surroundings when you can't see the details? Going is what kept him engaged.

He doesn't hold back. Honest and open, he wrestles with patience but does not hide how he feels. I watched him fearlessly hike down cliffs to surf uncrowded waves and navigate potentially awkward daily social situations with grace and charisma. He may have been on the backseat of the tandem, but Devon was driving the entire journey.

If I had to describe Devon one way after those two months on the road, it would be unabashedly himself. He showed up every day and gave it his all and beyond.

I went along to document what I knew would be an epic adventure. I got the photos I went looking for, but what I came home with was far greater. It changed the way I viewed life and its daily challenges. The trip gave me an appreciation of things that some may take for granted. It reminded me that a very important part of life is how you carry yourself through it, what you choose to put out there on a daily basis. Often life is lived in the small details of the day, how one chooses to treat others and navigate the challenges encountered time and time again.

Devon and I have grown incredibly close over the years. The bike trip was no doubt the catalyst for that. But numerous surf trips, snowboarding trips, and hours spent just hanging around his Bainbridge Island home have fostered a relationship that feels like blood. He went from being a guy that I knew of and was inspired by to a brother who inspires me for who he is and how he lives his life: in pursuit of his passions for authentic experiences with people and the outdoors.

With his lack of vision, there are things Devon can see that most people overlook.

Opposite: Goofing off—pretending to take a photo of Jeff while he takes a photo of me— on a seventy-five day, self-supported surf trip to Mexico via bicycle. 2013. *Jeff Hawe*

CHAPTER 1

This Is How I've Always Seen It

"Kneel down, keep your equipment beneath you and both hands on your snowboard!" our guide shouted. I felt the rotor wash, followed by a whirlwind of snow on my face, and then listened to the change in pitch the engine made as the helicopter pulled away from the peak.

I stood up and watched the chopper descend into the valley on the east side of the Cascade Range, and then tried to eye my own way down. The steep gullies were calling my name and their walls were begging to be slashed. Little pillow lines stood out like partially submerged boulders in a swift creek. I turned my back to the valley and began stomping down the snow to create a flat section in the pitch where I was standing. Then I lay my board down on the level bed and strapped into my binders. It was February 2006, and I was about to take my first heli-boarding run.

Ron Hendrickson, his brother Gary Hendrickson, and his son David stood nearby hooting with excitement and buckling their bindings as well. I looked at David and said, "Are you ready?" He was smiling ear to ear. A senior in high school, the kid was a ripping snowboarder, and I knew he would be right beside me all the way down. I wiggled my board into position, listened to the instructions from our guide Ken from North Cascade Heli Skiing, and prepared to drop after giving Ken a few seconds' head start.

Almost immediately, I passed our guide. The snow was smooth, bottomless, and with enough moisture to keep it stable throughout the steep sections. When I found a snow panel with significant pitch, I was able to make carving surf turns without the snow blowing out beneath my contact edge. The snow held, compacted nicely in my turns, and was still cold enough to keep me moving fast in the flat sections. It was perfection.

I rode through the trees and into the valley. I spotted the helicopter sleeping peacefully in the open snowfield and kept my board running flat on its base to maintain my speed as I rode through the valley floor. I took my board off and waited beneath the rotor blades as I looked back up at my line. David was right behind me, and he was riding in my track with speed and coming right at me. He threw up a little snow as he stopped and yelled, "That was awesome!" still smiling ear to ear.

In a minute we saw Ron, then Gary, and then Ken punch through the tree line, and all three of them rode up to where David and I stood grinning. "You were supposed to stay behind me," Ken scolded.

"I'm sorry, man, but this is a once-in-a-lifetime deal for me. I just can't slow down."

Ken initially looked bummed, but he seemed to understand my enthusiasm and softened. "OK, maybe we can move over to another area where I can safely see you guys from top to bottom."

"Thank you," I replied. "I really appreciate it. I don't want to be a pain, but it's just too good out there to stop midway down. Let's just meet up at the bottom instead."

Two days later, I walked through my front door in time for dinner and put my bags down on the hardwood floor of our living room. My ten-month-old daughter, Madrona, was crawling around in front of the fireplace. When she realized someone new had entered the room, she turned her head sideways and upward, then smiled and giggled. My wife, Rebecca, sat cross-legged on the floor next to her, glowing, and said, "Hey," as soon as I entered.

Leaving my bags where they fell, I took a seat on the couch near Rebecca, and soon Madrona began pulling herself up my shin and holding my knee for stability as she stood smiling at me. I felt like I was the most important man alive, absolutely sure of myself, and with a confidence that can only come from being responsible for the well-being of others.

Sitting on the couch, radiating with happiness, I looked at Rebecca and just smiled. She nodded and returned her gaze to Madrona, and I knew she understood how stoked I was. It had been a dream of mine since I began snowboarding twelve years earlier to be dropped off at the top of mountain peaks by a helicopter and then snowboard the untouched powder below. It was expensive. I was thirty-one years old, I had the money, and I finally rode in a helicopter for the first time. For two days I enjoyed perfect, smooth, untracked powder while being shuttled up and down by a flying machine I had mostly seen in war movies.

Time stood still in that moment and I thought, *This is it, Devon. This is how you have always seen it.*

I looked down at Madrona again, then around our living room. Our house was an old Tudor built in 1890, nestled on a safe, dead-end street in the historic district of Tacoma, Washington. In that moment, with my eyes on my baby girl, I said to myself, *This house is worth a good chunk of change and it's the only debt you have.* Still lost in my own prideful thoughts, I looked out the window at my truck, a new Chevy Silverado. It was parked next to Rebecca's freshly acquired silver Volkswagen Eurovan. My ego grew even bigger as I thought, *Those are paid for,* and then laughed.

Rebecca probably assumed I was silently enjoying the gratification of fatherhood as Madrona played at our feet, and she would have laughed at me in a big way if she knew how swollen my head was becoming over material things. Still, despite my shallow vanity, I had the most profound realization of my life on that couch. I realized, as I looked at it all, that for the first time ever I was completely happy, and 100 percent content. I could not think of anything more I wanted in that moment, or any part of my life I would change.

My brain shifted gears and I started looking at my life as a whole and the decisions I had made that put me in that happy place. I realized that many of the character traits I had been scolded for as a youth were now considered strengths as an adult. As far back as memory allowed, I could recall being labeled stubborn, defiant, energetic, and persistent.

Opposite: Getting my hands dirty framing our commercial building, which would later become YES Please! Coffee. Port Orchard, Washington. 2004. *Rebecca Raney*

I started examining specific decisions that had put me into my career and built my lifestyle. I dropped out of college after only a year to work in construction. It was a disappointing move to almost everyone around me, but I wanted to work outside, and I wanted to eventually own my own company. I wanted to feel tired at the end of the day and see tangible results from my labor. So I worked in as many of the trades as I could with the intent of becoming a home builder.

I roofed houses. Framed houses. Laid hardwood floors. I repaired plaster walls, installed interior trim, and put up exterior siding. My favorite work was always as a carpenter, and most of my time was spent in some aspect of that trade. My enthusiasm for building houses was recognized by Ron Hendrickson when we met for the first time in the spring of 2000, when I was twenty-four years old. He was a successful, second-generation builder and he would go on to mentor me for the next ten years.

Sitting on that couch in 2006, I reflected on how much I loved being a project manager for him. I also knew my time to branch out on my own was coming soon. I was ready, and I sat poised to start my own company in less than a year.

I continued to examine the decisions I made in my youth that seemed to disappoint so many people yet I knew had been the right moves for me. The sports I had given up, soccer and baseball, so I could ride my skateboard whenever I wanted and surf when the waves were good. Not many people understood why I had quit those team sports, but it was the right call for me, and I began to recount all the days I had spent surfing that year and all the evenings I went to the skate park on my way home from work. Recognizing that my life had been built around my passions, I smiled as I reminded myself of the main reason I started in the trades. Nodding quietly, I thought, *It's the freedom, Devon. You build houses for the flexible schedule you have.*

I had been lucky to meet up with my passions as a kid. I fell in love with the surf, the water, riding waves, and later riding any board I could get my hands on. As much as I loved it, though, I never wanted to be a pro skateboarder, a pro surfer, or a pro snowboarder. I have always wanted to keep my passions going strong on my own terms. As a kid, when I got bored with skateboarding, I would go surf. If surfing felt stale or the waves didn't show up, then I'd go back to getting sweaty and dirty on my skateboard. Sometimes I just rode my bike, or focused on the swim team. I always had a lot of energy, and I just liked adventure and doing stuff. From a young age, I was aware that the most important thing to me was my time and being in charge of how I spent it.

I must have had a dazed look on my face sitting on that couch for what felt like eternity as I thought about how happy I was. "Devon, hey! Let's eat," Rebecca said. Blinking my eyes, I looked at her and grinned as I stood and headed to the dinner table.

During our meal Rebecca asked what the snow was like, and how it felt to be a big shot who used a helicopter as a chairlift. As she teased me a little, I could tell she was slightly jealous, since she loves to snowboard too. The following month, it would be my turn to be jealous after Rebecca returned home from a luxury snowcat-chauffeured snowboarding trip to Baldface Lodge, where she rode perfect powder with a girlfriend. "It was perfectly smooth," I said. "It was easy to ride. I could have ripped that powder blindfolded." And I meant it, too. Neither of us knew how ironic that statement would become, so we just laughed and agreed how awesome good snow can be.

After the meal, I washed the dishes as Rebecca put Madrona down to sleep. My earlier feelings of pride and vanity had begun to fade, and in their place an unsettling sense of worry began to grow. I didn't know many people who were completely content, at least not many my age, and I wondered if I had peaked too soon. Maybe I had reached my goals at too young of an age and all that remained was complacency. Even more unnerving was the thought that I could go through the rest of my life without any challenges and therefore fall prey to the worst trap of all: mediocrity. I couldn't bear the thought and shook my head to rid myself of this doubt.

Before bed, I glanced at my calendar to see what the week ahead looked like. The housing market was booming and my week looked busy.

I checked my email and saw that I had confirmation from a man interested in buying my motorcycle. He would be picking the bike up that week. I would be sad to see it go.

I had acquired the bike as a result of a trip in 2005—an adventure, really—put together by a good friend of mine. He owned a vintage early-1970s BMW, and it was stored in Pennsylvania at the time, in his mother-in-law's garage. He was going to fly to the East Coast and ride the bike back across the country to Washington State. He asked if I wanted to join him on the ride, so I bought my 1999 BMW GS1100 sight unseen, online from a dealership in Wexford, Pennsylvania. I flew to Pennsylvania and met up with him, picked up my bike, and we spent the following two weeks riding west.

Looking at the email, I recalled how much fun the trip was. We had our skateboards, our sleeping bags, stoves, and a cooking pan. It was our intention to stay off any major highways and look for two-lane rural roads instead. Before we left, we researched the locations of skate parks along our route. Trying to find ramps and bowls in the most obscure places possible, we skated parks in towns I didn't even know existed.

We slept when we got tired, and wherever we felt like it. Each night was different in some cool way. We slept on the banks of the Mississippi, in farmers' fields, near lakes, and under the eaves of a bar at Yellowstone with Old Faithful in our line of sight during a rainstorm. One Wyoming night was spent sleeping inside one of the bowls at a skate park. They had just finished pouring the concrete that day, and as we lay in our sleeping bags, I could feel the warmth radiating from the concrete as a result of the chemical reaction caused by the cement hardening.

While sleeping on the beach of Lake Michigan, we were awoken by a park ranger. He spent an hour shining a flashlight in our eyes, calling us freeloaders and telling us we should be ashamed of ourselves for not using a proper campsite. Then he handed us tickets for $15 each. I remember thinking, *Dang. If I knew it was going to be this cheap I would have given him a twenty and gone back to bed.*

Sitting at my desk in Tacoma I thought, *It was the trip of a lifetime.* But was it? I wondered. The same friend and I had taken a similar motorcycle trip together in our early twenties and it had been amazing too. *They are all fun,* I thought.

I replied to the buyer's email and agreed to meet him later that week. I was bummed to sell the bike, but knowing that the

Opposite: Sleeping in the skate park. Wyoming. 2005. *Temple Cummins*

money would help buy a new ninety-horsepower outboard for our Boston Whaler softened the blow a bit. *All three of us can't ride on the motorcycle together,* I thought, *but we all enjoy being in the boat.* As I sat rationalizing my decision, I remembered what Rebecca had said: "You've already dropped that bike twice. You're a father now, and the motorcycle is dangerous." So I hit send on the reply and quit thinking about it.

As I got into bed, I thought over and over about the evening's revelation. I wanted to remember the night forever. It was hard to shut my brain off, and I stared at the ceiling as I tried to focus my thoughts on fun stuff. *March is coming,* I said to myself. This meant great snow in the mountains, as March always has lots of precipitation and is still cold. It had been a great winter, and I started drifting off to sleep as I thought about its highlights. I had competed in the Mount Baker Banked Slalom that winter. I was stoked on how I did, too, qualifying the first day and finishing in the upper half of my group for the finals. A lot of good snowboarders show up for that race. *I'd better ride more days next winter to be more prepared.*

———

By the summer of 2008, my dream had become a reality. I had left my job as project manager for Hendrickson Construction and formed Raney Group Construction. We were living in a house Rebecca had designed and I had built in Port Orchard, Washington—our construction company's first residential project.

Madrona was now three years old, and I was proud of the lifestyle that lay ahead of her: one full of adventure, time outdoors, days on the beach, and time in the snow. She was already learning to use the chairlift on her own at Mount Baker and showing an authentic love for that special place.

My year had been full of adventure. I had competed in the Mount Baker Banked Slalom again and pretty much posted the exact same result as the year before. I qualified on the first day and then placed just above the middle of my group in the finals. "At least you're consistent," a good friend of mine said to me. The summer before, I paddled the sixty-nine nautical miles from Sequim, Washington, east down the Strait of Juan de Fuca, then

At three years old, Madrona would ride up the Mount Baker rope tow goofy foot and slide back down regular foot. She eventually settled on regular foot as her preferred stance. Washington. 2008. *Rebecca Raney*

south into the Puget Sound and down to Bainbridge Island. I went with my usual adventure partner, Temple Cummins, and the two of us stuffed our kayaks with our skateboards, sleeping bags, stoves, and fishing poles. We slept on the beach whenever we got tired. On the evening of our first day we had paddled twenty-five miles and were exhausted. It was still warm, with no wind, and the sunset was shaping up to be memorable. Temple fished from his kayak in a kelp bed just offshore. Letting his lure drop to the bottom and then pulling it up to the surface, he caught a nice-sized lingcod. We took the fish straight to the beach, filleted it, removed the skin, and then rolled the meat in cornmeal. I fired up a stove and fried the fish in butter. Then we washed it down with a warm microbrew. To this day it remains one the best meals I have ever eaten.

In June, I opened an email from *From House to Home*, looked at the pictures, and read the article about our house and new business. During the interview I had discussed our company's mission statement, which focused on longevity. Reading the piece, I smiled when I reached a section where I gave kudos to Ron Hendrickson. "I didn't understand it until the end of my tenure with Ron, but as I grew into my own as a builder, I started to recognize that there were things I wanted to do to be environmentally friendly and green. I believe houses should be built to stand the test of time," they'd quoted me as saying.

I sat at my desk, reclined in my chair, and scrolled through beautiful photos of our home. They had been professionally staged, and they looked amazing. I read the text again and thought, *Wow, an article in year one.* I couldn't help but feel like my career path was paved in gold.

Two years had passed since I'd returned from heli-boarding and realized I was completely happy. I was still happy, but now I was beginning to feel invincible, too. Everything seemed to come easy now, and I credited the success to all the tough years I had as a kid, and the unique decisions I forced myself to make in order to create this lifestyle. Still, I was beginning to notice the numbing sensation of entitlement, and I wondered if my character was truly strong enough to remain intact with all this good fortune.

A month later, I opened another email from *From House to Home*. The editor was sad to inform me that, due to the plummeting real estate market and the looming recession expected to follow, her magazine was bankrupt. She went on to say that our issue would not go to print. However, the good news was that because they had already paid the photographer for his work, and the journalist for their words, we were free to keep the photos and the text.

I read the email again and said "bummer" out loud to no one in particular. Still, I was not that disappointed. The news had come during a time in my life when my optimism still had the resilience of granite.

That summer, I filled our freezer with local salmon and brought Madrona with me on every fishing excursion. She loved

Opposite: Living in the dream house Rebecca designed and I built; just before things fell apart. Manchester, Washington. 2008. *Jeff Hawe*

Wake up at four, take Madrona with me, walk down to the Boston Whaler, head out the mouth of Gig Harbor (less than a mile), and catch dinner. Good livin'. Washington. 2007. *Rebecca Raney*

being on the boat and was fascinated by the huge fish I brought to the surface and put in our net. Randomly, I entered my first fishing derby that August. The Point Defiance Anglers Club put on the event, and it cost $25 to enter. I figured, *What the heck, I'm out there every morning anyway,* and I ended up winning $500 by simply doing what I did every day in August. A twenty-pound king salmon headed for the Puyallup River put the money in my pocket and supplied the evening's barbeque, salmon cakes the following night, and teriyaki salmon bowls on the third evening.

As fall grew near, I focused my energy on surfing. In mid-September of 2008, I left for a quick three-day trip to northern Oregon with my friend Forrest Burki. The two of us surfed the beach breaks on the north coast and slept in my van at night.

On the second day, and after a long session surfing, I hit my head. Possibly because I was tired, or maybe just careless, I fell off the wave I was riding in an unusually awkward way. I dove slightly forward, and the curl rolled me up and then pushed me into the hard sand bottom headfirst. I felt my neck compress and I popped up to the surface in a panic. I went to the beach, sat for a while in the sand, and later the two of us drove back to Washington. The following day, my neck muscles were tight and felt sore and tender when I turned my head to either side. But within a few days the strain was gone, and everything seemed normal.

Less than two weeks later, I began to notice some trouble with my vision. I was at the skate park in Gig Harbor, Washington, riding the bowls and enjoying the exercise, when I saw lightning bugs all around me. It was four in the afternoon and fully light out, and I became confused as my brain ruled out the possibility of lightning bugs. I would remain confused for quite a while.

Any concern I had that my life was too easy and without sufficient challenges, or that my career path was paved in gold, would shortly be silenced forever. Soon enough, I would be again relying on the character traits I had developed as a kid. Words like "stubborn," "defiant," "energetic," and "persistent" would take on yet even more meaning as I fought for my family, my passions, my place in this world, and a new way to exist in my daughter's life.

CHAPTER 2

I Want to Marry You

In the spring of 1995, shortly before I turned twenty, I moved to Gig Harbor, Washington, to be with my family. My parents, Dave and Pam Raney, and both of my younger siblings, my brother Blake and sister Laura, had relocated to Gig Harbor from Valencia, California, during the fall of 1993.

I had stayed back in Valencia to attend my first year at a small conservative Christian college. My high school girlfriend was going there—her father was a teacher at the school—and so she filled out an application for me as well. It was the only college application sent out on my behalf, and so I followed her to a place I knew very little of.

I hated my experience at the school from the beginning. When my girlfriend broke up with me halfway through the year, I used it as an excuse to stop going to class and spent all my time skateboarding instead. Soon I was failing college.

I shared a dorm room with a guy named Scott Gravatt, and he was the only positive thing that came out of my time in college. Scott was a skateboarder, and since both of us had mentioned our love of skating in our registration paperwork we were hooked up as roommates. We were the only two skateboarders enrolled, and we became close friends and remain so today.

It was a challenging year, and the low moments were intensified by the fact that my family had moved up to Washington State.

I had not been to see their new home and had no idea what life was like for my brother and sister.

In the summer I took a job doing construction on campus. Both Scott and I stayed in our dorm and began doing repair work on brick walls, plaster repair on buildings, and general paint maintenance. We were the only two guys on our floor that summer and we had a great time. On my days off, I stayed up in Ventura for the surf with friends or my grandparents.

In the fall, school started again and I was not enrolled. I bounced around on couches and tried to get a foothold in a construction trade. As the year went on, I missed my family more and more. I tried to find my joy in surfing and skateboarding. During the holidays, I asked my folks if I could move to Gig Harbor and live with them. They were not happy with the choices I had been making, but they agreed. For the next three years, I struggled to fit into my new life in Washington: finding new friends and getting established in construction.

I met Rebecca Storset during Labor Day weekend in 1998 at a retreat for college students I was attending with my brother Blake. Rebecca was born and raised in Gig Harbor and although she and my brother had attended different high schools in town, they had mutual friends and knew each other. Rebecca had a boyfriend at the time, and she and I said very little to each other during the retreat.

Toward the end of September, I crossed paths with Rebecca at the Puyallup Fair. She was with her boyfriend again and I was with my brother. We stood around and talked for a while longer this time, and I learned that Rebecca was staying home to attend community college for a year because of some tragic family circumstances. She was looking for a job, and I casually mentioned Northwest Snowboards, where I had worked off and on for the previous two years. "I'll put in a good word for you," I said. Then, just in case she was wondering when she would see me again, I rattled off, "But I am not working there right now because I'm headed to Canada to work as a carpenter at a Young Life camp called Malibu during their off-season. I won't be back until January." Rebecca didn't seem concerned with my return date, but she was grateful for the job connection and worked at the snowboard shop for a brief time.

In mid-January of 1999, I ran into Rebecca again. I had been trying to find her since the moment I got back into town. I was hoping for a casual crossing of paths so that I could pretend that I wasn't thinking about her constantly and driving all over town hoping I would see her somewhere. Finally, I got lucky when I stopped at the coffee shop in town for a latte. Rebecca stood in the back of the store, smiling and looking relaxed. Everything seemed to be glowing. I blinked, tried to focus, and wondered if I should order a drink.

It was on that day that I truly saw her for the first time. She looked a little bohemian in her green corduroy pants and tight sweater. Her purse hung across her chest and one hand rested on the top of the small bag. Her hair was down past her shoulders and blond at the tips. She looked right at me and I walked directly over. We talked for a while, filling each other in on the past four months. Then I got down to business. "So, you guys broke up? I'm sorry to hear that. Well, what are you doing tomorrow?" I asked.

From then on, the two of us hung out together all the time. She was never in a hurry and had a quiet confidence about her. She made me feel like she was content with whatever we were doing. She didn't mind stopping by the skate park and she seemed to enjoy watching me skate. She was an artist with a painted mural on the front of her VW Beetle, and when we listened to music, I would buy albums I had never heard of but hoped to impress her with. Everything she did impressed me. I waited all the way until April before I kissed her. It wasn't long before I knew I was in love.

Later that spring, I bought two tickets for a Greg Brown concert. He was playing in Portland, Oregon, 200 miles south of Gig Harbor. Rebecca was always game for adventure, and I knew she would enjoy the city's laid-back vibe. It was going to be our first road trip, and it would be our first official date—this outing would cost money, have a start time, involve a meal, and provide the chance to wear more than jeans and a T-shirt. When I asked Becca to go, she sounded super excited, which was nice, and then said, "My friend Catharine wants to go too. Can we get her a ticket?" I was a little bummed at first. I had a design of my own making, and it didn't include Catharine. But I got over it. I would do anything to hang out and have a good time with Rebecca. I told her, "She can have my ticket and I'll buy one at the door."

Greg Brown is a folksinger and a poet. Like all young lovers, Rebecca and I had our mood music, and Greg Brown was our guy. It felt as if every song was for our benefit. He sang with a deep voice and to the twang of an old guitar. Later, when we got married, we danced the official slow song to our favorite Greg Brown tune, "Hey Baby Hey." It remains one of my only clear memories of that night, which registers, in the best way, as an elated blur in my mind. Married now for seventeen years, we eventually changed out the CD, but on occasion, Greg Brown still makes a comeback.

We drove to Portland in my 1984 Volvo 240 Turbo Wagon. It was sleek and black, and I loved driving that car. Rebecca would tease me many years later, saying, "You were a lot more relaxed when you had that Volvo." I believe stylish cars of a vintage model make a person drive more chill. My old Volvo sure had that effect on me.

Arriving nearer to the start time than I had planned as a result of my chill car, we hurried to the ticket booth. "One ticket, please," I said.

The gal behind the window smiled really big, and I thought maybe something lucky was going to happen. Then she said, "Sold out, man."

To my satisfaction, Rebecca looked a little more disappointed than I expected. Which made it easier to act excited for her and Catharine. I said, "You guys go, it'll be super fun."

Hesitant, Becca asked, "How will we find you?"

Since this was in the days before cell phones, she had a valid concern. I responded, "I'll walk around Portland and be at the car when you get out."

After telling my prospective girlfriend to go on and enjoy our first date without me, I started walking into the city. My first stop was some dinner. Solo and nursing my wounds, I treated myself to an above-budget meal, followed by a microbrew. Then I started walking again.

It wasn't long before the disappointment faded and I was enjoying my tour of Portland. I made sure to connect with the historic North Park greenbelt located in the center of the city. Then I left, taking a different street back toward the venue. This was my "outa town" technique for not covering any ground twice. The old buildings were really what I enjoyed looking at.

I was getting cold, and a little tired. I came to a building that was eye-catching but out of place. Looking like a small castle, with lots of pillars, stairs, and marble, it had a sign out front that read: "FREE IQ TEST." I went up to the door for a closer look. The building belonged to the Church of Scientology. I peered in; everything looked warm, and since I had overspent my budget on dinner, free anything sounded pretty great, so I went inside.

After I entered the lobby, a woman mysteriously appeared out of nowhere. I learned quickly that she was a Scientologist. As she shared her zeal with hungry, cultish eyes, it was obvious the woman had thought she'd solved the impossible questions surrounding the meaning of our existence—she knew the "Truth." She asked me if I knew anything about the Church of Scientology, and I replied, "I heard Tom Cruise is a member."

She did not laugh. *Maybe she doesn't like Tom*, I thought. After she asked how she could help me, I happily replied, "I'm here for the free IQ test." She directed me to a warm, cozy corner of the room and told me she would be right back.

Soon I was seated at a desk with a pencil and paper, working out problems and answering questions that didn't make much sense. Midway through, I wondered what score Tom Cruise got. Finishing quickly, I thought, *Maybe I can get bonus points for speed.* I sat at the desk for a while—it was warm inside, and I didn't want to leave.

After the lady returned and collected my test and pencil, we stood there awkwardly, staring at each other in silence. Eventually she spoke first: "Would you like to wait for the result?" Wondering if she planned on mailing it, I responded to the stupid question dryly: "Yes, I would like the result." My response seemed to please her. As she walked away, I braced myself for the tour, followed by the sales pitch to convert to Scientology, that would surely follow her discovery of my high score. I decided I would not reject her faith until after I learned how brilliant I was.

She returned sooner than expected, and I figured this must have meant there were no wrong answers for her to mark. As she stood in front of me, I noticed her eyes had lost some of their feverish zeal and she didn't seem as eager to give me the tour as she was a minute ago. Clearing her throat, she said, "Your IQ is 90."

Instantly I asked, "Is that for the first half?"

Talking slowly now, for my benefit, she said, "No, 90 is the total. Do you know what the points mean?"

Nodding, I said, "Yes." But in truth I only knew my score was low. I had no idea what it meant on her scale.

Standing there uncomfortably while she stared at me like I was a puppy, I waited for her to say something reassuring. She just kept staring and I wondered to myself, *Does she think I am retarded?* Soon, my active brain began to derail.

Abruptly I broke the silence and said, "Thank you for your time."

In defiance of all things Scientology, I put a little swagger in my step and walked out of there with the coolness of someone who hadn't just learned he had a double-digit IQ.

Walking back to the concert venue, my immediate thought, *I guess I won't be working at NASA anytime soon,* was followed by, *This can't be right. My parents said I was brilliant.*

Laughing at the discovery of my small mind, I realized my low IQ went a long way toward explaining some of the stuff I did in high school. After taking some comfort that I now had stupidity to blame for some of my actions, I started to worry. *My low IQ will surely restrict my future job options and hopes of having a family. But maybe a family is out of the question anyway, since no woman will want me around if I can't help the kids with their math homework once they enter middle school.*

So I walked on, with the dark cloud of mental incapacity above me. I showed up at the parking lot before the ladies came out of the event. My mood lightened when the gals reached the car and started telling stories from the show. Rebecca asked how my night was. "Great," I said with way too much stoke. "I ate some good food and had a beer."

Becca asked for more details but I was vague, always shifting the conversation back to Greg Brown. *I really love this woman,* I thought to myself, but how could the following statement bode well for me? *I want to ask for your hand in marriage, but a recent IQ test indicates our future might be limited.*

Shaking the thought, I tried to focus on being smart while driving us out of Portland. Sounding brilliant, I said, "Look at all the Portland lights. It must take thousands of kilowatts to light this city."

The babes sat silently in response.

I lay in bed that night and overanalyzed my evening's test result. Since I had left in such a hurry it was impossible to understand the reason it was so low. I didn't believe it was accurate. It felt weird from the start. Then I laughed out loud as I recalled the only other IQ test I had ever taken. Then I considered how truly different the two results were. Drifting off to sleep, I said to myself, *Devon, testing has never been a friend to you.*

I had taken an IQ test in the fifth grade. It had not been mandated by my school, but rather by my mom. She had me taking lots of tests back then, and I completed them all: reading assessments, math quizzes, puzzles, riddles, crosswords, and maybe even the entrance exam for the United States Army.

My mom informed me that the result of the IQ test was 138 points, which meant I was gifted. I believe she was more excited than I ever was. Any joy I felt came from firmly believing I would no longer have to do homework. I remember hoping my principal had already heard the news and was passing on my IQ points to the governor, who would naturally pardon me from middle school.

Informing an eleven-year-old kid with a defiant spirit that he is gifted is probably not a good idea. You might as well give him a trust fund with a million dollars and then still hope he gets a job and develops a work ethic. Why would anyone get a job if he had a million bucks? Why would I ever need to study again if I was gifted?

Who knows, maybe something was fishy about my fifth-grade test as well. What I do know for sure is that validating my intelligence with a point rating was not a good thing for me. At a young age I no longer felt the need to study. Naturally, I assumed I would ace my exams while I breezed through school. My assumption was wrong. When I stopped doing the work, not only did my grades suffer but my scholastic experience diminished as well. Being told I was smart made me lazy.

Fortunately for my future as an adult, an aptitude test for passion does not exist. The important things cannot be tested, and so I was under no false pretense that I would be breezing through my professional career or on cruise-control as a husband and father. Tenacity and courage are not measured by a point system. As a young man, I was ready to prove myself, and so I put my grit to the test in the arena of life, and not in the classroom.

Rebecca recognized my enthusiasm for living, and she believed in me. If there is any real proof that I am intelligent, it lies in the simple fact that I didn't let her get away. I never told Rebecca about my odd choice to walk in for a late-night IQ test, and I certainly didn't tell her my result. As time went on, I realized more and more how brilliant she is, and figured I had little to gain by revealing my own dim wit.

She said "yes," and we got married on December 19, 1999, less than a year after our night in Portland. I was twenty-four years old and she was twenty. Surprisingly, none of our family or friends objected to our decision. I figured the move would be a shocker because of the social pressure to wait until after college or until we had careers. But people around us seemed to know it was the right thing for us.

The first thing I had noticed about Rebecca was her fierce independence. She was the only person I had ever met who simply had no expectation that the world owed her anything or that she would be magically taken care of. Rebecca had a healthy counterculture approach to life, and I remember fondly when she told me about the time she and a friend moved by themselves to Seaside, Oregon, as high-schoolers.

Rebecca had just finished the eleventh grade, and so naturally she packed up her VW Beetle and left for the beach. Her best friend, Cressa, sat beside her in the passenger seat. They were seventeen years old and looking for a new level of adventure. The two girls found a month-to-month studio rental on the seedy side of town and paid the rent in cash. The fact that their landlord was aware of their age, that they were still in high school, and then kept their agreement under the table is the biggest indicator of how sketchy their environment was. Both girls applied at the Shilo Inn and began working as front-desk receptionists. They didn't spend the summer partying or getting wild. Instead, they played beach volleyball and saved most of their paychecks. The adventure gave them a glimpse of the freedom most don't see until later in life, and it would not have been possible without a willingness to take a risk.

Throughout our engagement and into our early years of marriage, I remember Rebecca often saying to me, "Our future is wide open and we can do anything we choose to do as long as we do it together." It was an idealistic approach during a time when our lives were uncomplicated, but her statement would prove to be more prophetic than either of us could have known at the time. Getting married young is probably the best decision I have ever made. I had no idea what a lifetime together looked like, and I didn't know if I would ever become an actual adult. But I didn't feel like Rebecca knew those things either. Neither of us owned a credit card back then nor had any established credit history. I was running a balance of minus seventeen dollars in my bank account and hadn't carried car insurance in more than a year. Young and without any money or an established career, I did not embody the traditional definition of an adult, but I was confidently ready for a lifetime with Rebecca and the loyalty it required.

We moved onto a sailboat and started living life full speed ahead. We made the decision together to buy the boat as an alternative to paying rent, but it was Rebecca who had the money for our down payment. The vessel was a 1979 twenty-seven-foot Catalina with an old nine-horsepower outboard motor. The boat cost $9,000 and we paid for it by qualifying for our first loan together. Our payment was $127 a month. Not long after that, I reinstated my car insurance and realized I might become an adult after all.

Two years later, we built our first house on a piece of waterfront land on Washington State's Puget Sound. The lot looked to the southwest, with enough elevation gain to see for miles, and in the evenings the sun would set behind three beautiful madrona trees. This sunset, framed by the powerful madronas, was our television screen every evening for the four years we lived there.

Rebecca and I loved that land. Our fondness was always intensified by the sense of achievement that came from doing things our way. We had done our best to save money for it by living on the sailboat, and it was the first house Rebecca and I built on our own from start to finish. Rebecca was completing her bachelor's degree at the University of Washington, with a minor in architecture. She drew the blueprints of our 1,400-square-foot house and

Opposite: A beautiful bride at my side during a time when everything was a little simpler. Tacoma Union Station, Washington. 1999. *Raney Family Collection*

Madrona trees out in front of the first house Rebecca and I built. Gig Harbor, Washington. 2003. *Rebecca Raney*

I built almost all of it with my own hands. Many of our interior finishes were picked up at a secondhand store in Seattle.

The juxtaposition of such a simple house on such a premium piece of property was almost magical. It was humble and serene, and the little house seemed perfectly placed, almost unnoticeable or like it had always been there. Rebecca and I developed a deep appreciation for our madrona trees, and no matter how busy our schedules were, we took a moment every evening to stare at them.

Nearly three years later, on April 16, 2005, our daughter was born. We named her Madrona.

Madronas are native to the Pacific Northwest. Our daughter's full name is Madrona Adelle Raney and her initials spell MAR, the Spanish word for sea. She was, in part, given her name because Rebecca and I love the tree, but in a larger way, her name comes from that very special place and time in our marriage when we would spend our evenings looking at those three trees.

Northwest madronas don't survive unless they are within fifty miles of salt water. I thought this was awesome. As a lifelong surfer, I felt it was fitting to impose a coastal living clause at birth. To this day I tease my Madrona with the reminder that if she ever moves farther than fifty miles from the salt water, not only will I not visit, but she might have a tough time surviving.

When Madrona was born, Rebecca labored in delivery with the assistance of a midwife at a birthing center in Tacoma, not far from where we lived in Gig Harbor. Since it was a Saturday, outside of regular hours, the clinic was locked up, and we waited in the parking lot for the midwife to arrive. "Maybe she got lost," I said sarcastically. "She's not lost, she is late," Rebecca growled. "I need to stand up. Pop the top of the van," she said. I pushed up the roof of our VW Weekender and slid the overhead mattress out of the way. Wiping the beads of sweat from my brow, I asked nervously, "At what point should I drive to the hospital?"

Rebecca paced in circles in the van. "There she is, there she is!" Rebecca moaned with relief.

I watched Rebecca labor for nine hours, drug free, before our baby girl showed her head. Then I heard someone yell my name. "Devon, get your shirt off. Skin to skin, Daddy, skin to skin!" the midwife bellowed. Frantically I ripped off my tee, wondering if I might faint. "The most powerful connection a father can make during the delivery period is immediately after the baby comes out," the midwife reminded me.

"Oh yes, that's right," I mumbled. Overwhelmed, I started processing the now rapidly unfolding scene as a series of shouts and screams. "Ahhhh!" someone yelled. *I think that's Rebecca*, I thought. "Get ready, Devon!" followed from a different voice. *She should be a football coach.* Then another "Ahhhh!" from my wife, and finally I heard Coach scream, "Here she is. Skin to skin, Papa!"

Someone threw a slimy bundle of responsibility right into my arms and I pulled her tight to my bare chest. The tears welled up in my eyes, I stared at my little girl, and I don't remember hearing anything else.

CHAPTER 3

Red Herring

My doctor visits began almost immediately after I saw lighting bugs all around me that day at the skate park. It was near the end of October 2008, six weeks after I'd hit my head on the sand while surfing in Oregon. I was no longer able to recognize the faces of the people I loved, read a book, or see myself in the mirror. I knew at that point I should have stopped driving completely, but I continued doing so on back roads and at slow speeds for another month until the end of November, when I drove off the side of the road and hit a dog. Ashamed, fearful, and defeated, I never drove again. Months later, I exchanged my driver's license for an identification card.

At first, doctors mentioned a possible brain tumor, and so we tracked that path and ruled it out. Then multiple sclerosis became the focus until another normal MRI eliminated that possibility. I was having a hard time finding a doctor who could explain why my eyesight was becoming pixelated, waxy, smudgy, and less usable on a daily basis.

In the exam room of Dr. Steven Hamilton, with my eyes dilated once again, I tried to count in my head how many doctors I had seen since the accident. Three months ago my eyes had never been dilated. Now, I had gotten used to the sensation. I was beginning to expect each new doctor to fail, unable to diagnose my condition.

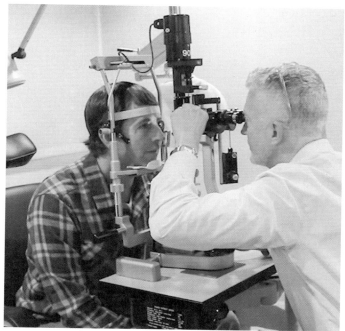

Dr. Stephen Hamilton examines my optic nerves. Seattle, Washington. *Rebecca Raney*

Although I was getting used to disappointment, I still had hope. So I forced myself to have an open mind and to hope this new doctor might perform a miracle. Dr. Hamilton is a Seattle neuro-ophthalmologist recognized globally for his research and publications on optic neuropathy. A University of California, Irvine School of Medicine grad who did a fellowship at Harvard, he has won Seattle Top Doctor and Regional Top Doctor awards more than once. Dr. Hamilton rearranged his yearlong new-patient wait list so he could see me. I knew that my strange symptoms—the ones other doctors couldn't figure out—were the reason I'd moved to the front of the line. At first, the urgency of the attention I was getting made me uneasy, then panic-stricken.

I counted in my head the number of times I had been in for an MRI or CT scan during the past three months. The tally reminded me of the constant stream of medical bills I was paying. Then my panic turned to anger at myself, for choosing the cheapest individual healthcare plan. The huge group plans weren't offered to me when I started my own company, and my individual plan had a high deductible and no dental or vision coverage.

I could tell as soon as he entered the room that Dr. Hamilton was on a different level than the other doctors I had been seeing. He had a confidence that was natural and authentic. It was not the falsely inflated confidence meant to put me at ease that I had grown accustomed to lately. I was relaxed during his examination of my eyes and optic nerves. I never felt rushed; he spent two hours examining with me.

We engaged in small talk during the first part of the exam, but I knew he was getting to his diagnosis by the tone change in his voice. "Well," he said, "it may just be a red herring."

"What does that mean?" I asked sheepishly.

"A red herring is something that throws us off the trail, because the obvious diagnosis seems too easy," he replied. "In this case it's the odds, which would mean you are a rare case if in fact you have what I think could be the cause."

He went on to explain that all my symptoms were pointing to an optic nerve disorder called Leber's hereditary optic neuropathy (LHON). Because it's so rare, doctors usually don't even consider it. Standard practice is to look for a more common diagnosis first.

He could sense my concern. "Don't worry just yet. Let's order the DNA test and go from there."

I didn't have a clue what "rare" meant in his world. "What are the odds that I have it?" I asked.

"It's very rare," Dr. Hamilton replied. "One person in eight hundred thousand. I have only seen a few LHON patients in my time."

We sat in silence as Rebecca drove us home. It went without saying that Dr. Hamilton was the most knowledgeable doctor we had seen. Still, we had just left another appointment without a diagnosis.

My mind seemed to be cracking under the weight of not knowing. The struggle to keep from wondering about all the things that could possibly be wrong with my eyes or body was almost unbearable. Still, even more unbearable was the hope that I could wake up one morning and everything would be normal again. One way or another, good or bad, I needed an answer.

Staring out the car window, I was confident that I would not test positive for LHON. The odds were too strong against it. Regardless, I would continue to see Dr. Hamilton until he figured out what was wrong.

Next spread: Mount Baker, Washington, in all its glory. *Colin Wiseman*

CHAPTER 4

Down the Hill from Baker

A couple of weeks later, I stood in the parking lot of Mount Baker, Washington, on the passenger side of my truck, which had really become Becca's truck by that point, and fumbled with my avalanche beacon. It had snowed thirteen inches overnight, the temperature was abnormally low—in the teens—and December was acting like it did in the midnineties when I'd learned to snowboard. My friend Mike Cummins, Temple's brother, stood next to me, already suited up, in a hurry to buy his ticket and heckling me to speed things up.

My phone rang at 8:30 a.m. Normally I would let the phone go unanswered per the unspoken rules of a powder day, but I took the call. I had been waiting daily for news, and in a minute it would come, in the infallible form of a DNA test result.

I answered and went through the formalities of "hello" and "good morning." The nurse told me my recent test had come back positive for the genetic disorder Leber's hereditary optic neuropathy.

I abruptly asked, "Will I go blind?"

"Yes," she said, after a slight pause.

Embarrassed before the words left my mouth, I blurted, "But he told me the odds were one in eight hundred thousand!" She remained silent, and I knew it was not her place to explain.

"Dr. Hamilton would like to talk with you in person," she said, "and can make space for you today any time you can come in." I thanked her for the worst news I had ever received, then told her we were on our way.

Mike and Rebecca heard it all. I don't remember our exchange of words, but Mike gave me a hug. Rebecca was already taking off her snow gear while getting in the driver's seat of our truck. I removed my beacon and took my place in the passenger seat.

The two of us drove down the hill in silence, until Becca broke it with a tearful voice. "I am so sorry," she said. "I don't want this to happen to you."

I had never heard her refer to me in the singular like that before. For an instant, it was one of the loneliest moments of my life, as I began to see myself alone, with the inevitable darkness looming. I struggled to shake that thought and looked over at Rebecca. With a tight chest and holding back tears, I said, "To *us*, baby, you didn't want it to happen to us."

Twenty minutes later we stopped at our condo, a six-month rental in a complex called Snowater in a town called Glacier. Rebecca and I changed out of our snow gear and walked a few units down the way to pick up Madrona. She was spending the first half of the morning at Temple's condo, and hanging with his son, her buddy Cannon. I told Temple about the call while Rebecca picked up Madrona.

It was Friday, December 19, 2008, the day of our ninth wedding anniversary. Although the conditions were great for snowboarding on the mountain, it was the worst snowstorm Seattle and the lowlands had seen in 127 years. I had already heard about the chaos from people in the parking lot who had driven up from the city that morning.

We drove in silence mostly, and I have no real memory of Madrona being in the car. She had always been a patient child, but I believe she was more quiet than usual because she could sense the weight of our situation, watching with the intuition only a child possesses.

We pulled onto the I-5 freeway and the silence gave way to the heavy crunching sound our tires made in the deep tracks carved out by other vehicles. It was cold, with two feet of snow on the ground, and a high-pressure system had moved in to clear the skies. Rebecca said there was a low haze over the farmland. Moving through such a beautiful landscape, while on a mission to discuss bad news, gave me a strange feeling. I didn't know how to feel, and I thought it might be the literal definition of surreal.

Staring out the window, I went over and over the whirlwind of events that had started three months earlier when I bounced my head off the bottom while surfing in Oregon. I was thirty-three years old, in the best shape of my life, had just built our dream home, and was planning to ride powder all winter with my family at Baker.

I looked over at Becca. She was driving with unusual resolution. The determination was obvious in her posture and I knew the effort was for me. I did not need to see her clearly to know how beautiful she was in that instant. I did not look back at my daughter. My neck would not turn; my body refused to let me look back at my child because my brain was not ready to absorb all the loss I believed was coming.

I had everything I wanted, dreamed of, and worked for at that moment in my life. The emotion from earlier in the day was gone now; I felt nothing. Like a farmer who watches with blank expression as a fire rips through his crops, I knew my world was burning down.

In all the years I had lived in Washington State, there had never been snow that deep in the I-5 corridor. Arriving in Seattle, Rebecca described a Metro bus that had punched through a guardrail, with its front end hanging out over the freeway at the end of a steep street in the Capitol Hill district.

Rebecca took the next exit and got off downtown. I called the doctor's office and they told us to come right over. Once inside we were greeted enthusiastically, and instead of being directed to the waiting room, we were escorted immediately to an exam room. The special attention made me feel important, and then uneasy, like I was being served my favorite meal right before going to the electric chair.

Dr. Hamilton came in and I was immediately grateful for his professionalism and genuine compassion. He started by giving me contact info for two people he knew of in Washington who also had Leber's hereditary optic neuropathy. He suggested that I contact them and learn their stories; maybe their experiences would help me adjust to my new life. I saw how sincere he was being, how wise his words were, yet I dismissed them in less than a second. "Let's move on," I said flatly.

We began our long discussion about my diagnosis. Beginning with the numerical code of my DNA, he explained what "genetic" meant. Numb, and in a haze, I heard fragments only. Confusion turned to fear when I heard him say, "Generally, patients with LHON do very well. Most cases I am aware of are high functioning and still able to hold a job and contribute to society."

I heard this sentence and something seemed to twist inside of me.

"Have you considered enrolling in the Seattle's Lighthouse for the Blind school?" he asked.

I let his question sink in. I suppose most people probably do some research at home and have a general overview of their situation prior to the visit. I did not do any research, and Dr. Hamilton was obviously unaware that I had been spending all my time snowboarding instead.

Why would I study up on being blind, I thought, *when I could use my last days of eyesight ripping powder with my family?*

I did not even know a school for the blind existed. The gravity of my situation began to settle in and then turned to shock. I sat silent, almost as if he were talking to someone else and I was just observing.

Finally I spoke. "Does my daughter carry the gene?" I asked. Before he could answer, I blurted, "Can she lose her eyesight?"

Dr. Hamilton explained that LHON is a mitochondrial disorder. Since mitochondria DNA is passed on from the mother, not the father, I could not have passed the gene to Madrona. My body felt lighter with the news. The battle would be mine to fight. I felt pain for Rebecca, who I knew would fight beside me, but our daughter, our beautiful daughter, would never live in fear of going blind. It was hard to hear that my brother and my sister also have the genetic disorder, but he was clear to say that as adults, they would most likely never lose their eyesight. He said, "In your case, Devon, the trauma to your head caused by your surfing accident most likely triggered the manifestation."

We learned a lot during that visit, almost too much. Dr. Hamilton was never in a rush and answered all our questions in detail. Finally, I found the courage to ask the question I was scared to know the answer to. "Will my eyes go completely black?" I blurted out. There was a pause. I could tell he was being careful with his response. "Most people with LHON keep their peripheral vision intact," he finally replied.

Dr. Hamilton explained that the center of my optic nerve was dying, but the sidewalls of that nerve would remain healthy, as they are a separate system of fibers. "There is nothing wrong with your eyeballs," he said. "The center of your optic nerve is dying and no longer receives the transmission. This is why your vision now has the huge dark mass, or absent space, but you can still bring in certain things on the side." Explaining what that meant, he went on to say that I should only lose my central vision. Central vision is detail vision, considered the usable portion, and its loss is a significant insult to the body's senses. I learned the different ways the word "blind" is used. Fortunately for me, sideways vision is the baseline for movement in athletics and would prove to be a bigger asset than I expected.

I didn't think there was possibly anything more to discuss when Dr. Hamilton said, "You may want to apply for Social Security Disability." Knowing what I did for a career, and that I made a good living, he continued by saying, "It will help until you figure out what you can do again."

Horrified, I stared at him like he was urinating on my shoes. *What?* I thought. *I can do anything I put my mind to, but I choose to build houses. Is this dude for real? Grandpa would get out of his grave and whoop my ass if I took a disability check.*

Denial blocked my mind from comprehending, or even hearing, what Dr. Hamilton was saying as he laid out the tools and programs he believed would help. "Acceptance" was not a word I was familiar with yet, but just one year later I would visit the Lighthouse School for the Blind with the intention of attending. I decided against it at the last minute because I was not willing to spend that much time away from my family.

Rebecca must have seen the wheels spinning in my head, because she broke the awkward silence by graciously thanking Dr. Hamilton. Following her lead, I did the same. Agreeing to visit again in six months and retest my field of vision, we said good-bye.

It was dark when we left the office. Sitting in the truck, Rebecca said, "Where should we go?" I looked over at her. "I don't want to go home," I said. It was only a thirty-minute ferry ride to get to our house across the water from Seattle.

Rebecca was reluctant to drive the 114 miles back up to Glacier while the conditions worsened at the tail end of the biggest blizzard Seattle had seen in over a century. She said, "It will be a white-knuckle drive."

But home had become a sad place. I had begun to spend evenings sitting in a chair and staring across the bay at the city lights. In the darkness, I would watch as planes flew across the night sky while their blinking lights disappeared in the center of my vision. Each night it was worse; I used the blinking lights as a way to gauge the deterioration of my vision. Rebecca did not like watching me sit alone, removed, and measuring the loss.

Rebecca looked at me then, and said, "I think we should stay up at Baker as much as we can."

Mount Baker was where we felt safe. We both knew we could not hide forever, but we chose to spend as much time as possible there that winter. Away from our busy life, we let our uncertain future settle in slowly.

The drive back to Glacier did not disappoint, proving to be a white-knuckler. We drove in silence again, only this time we felt a small sense of relief knowing the search for a diagnosis was over. For the first time since I had begun seeing blurry spots three months earlier, I slept peacefully through the night. In the morning we went snowboarding without any expectations, and with the intention of riding together for as long as we possibly could.

Next spread: Following my daughter and stealing her style—or maybe she stole mine. Either way, I am a happy dad at the 2018 Dirksen Derby. Mount Bachelor, Oregon. *Colin Wiseman*

CHAPTER 5

Tandem Snowboarding

For the duration of December 2008 I continued to snowboard on my own. By mid-January my eyesight had deteriorated to a low enough level for me to begin questioning whether I should be snowboarding at all. Each morning as I loaded the chairlift, I wondered if I might end up hospitalized, and in a morbid way I felt prepared for that outcome.

Four months remained on our condo rental agreement, and when it terminated some decisions would need to be made. Rebecca and I walked gingerly around the topic of moving out and avoided mentioning "our future" completely. Most days, the countdown felt like a looming time bomb.

The two of us intentionally communicated daily, but generally kept our discussions light. We both felt an undercurrent of anxiety and avoided the biggest conversation completely. The elephant in the room was ignored while we said things like, "Will we need two cars now?" What we really wanted to address but were too fearful to talk about was, "If I can't build houses, how are we going to survive without my income?" *How were we going to make money?*

Before my accident, I had a proposal out to a couple from Gig Harbor and hoped to sign a deal to build them a waterfront home. At the point when I stopped driving, I gave the pair the news of my diagnosis and they understandably moved on. I hadn't earned a penny in over eight months.

Our sixth-month rental in Glacier and our passes at Baker had been paid for in full earlier that fall. Although the big-ticket items had been covered, we were paying for daily expenses with borrowed money from a line of credit I had established for our construction company, and we leveraged our primary residence as collateral on that loan. The money was going out fast, but we had not yet reached the point our debt would be greater than our equity.

It felt foolish to continue dodging conversations about money, and finally Rebecca said, "I'm going to manage the coffee shop. We are going to find a way to grow sales so I can pull a salary our family can live on."

Rebecca impressed me with her leadership in that moment. It was what we needed for movement in any direction, and I said, "Alright, let's figure it out." Her suggestion was one that I could never have made. I wanted to work, I loved to work, and I was still holding on to the delusion that soon I would be driving again, building houses again, and providing for the family.

In 2003, we had purchased commercial land in Port Orchard, Washington, in a fifty–fifty partnership with my parents. The real estate market was growing out of control at the time, but I could see a decline on the horizon. I felt it was important to diversify, and a light commercial project was the most viable option. My parents agreed. It felt like an honor to reach the point in life where my parents saw me as a financial resource and no longer a risk.

Rebecca had graduated cum laude from the University of Washington with a bachelor of fine arts, and a minor in architecture. She had spent her entire work experience as a barista, which gave her a strong sense of coffee bar work flow and efficiency, and she drew a blueprint for a double-sided drive-through coffee shop that came together flawlessly in the field. I still consider that commercial construction project to be the finest professional achievement Rebecca and I have experienced.

Once the coffee shop was open, Rebecca intended for a full-time manager to oversee daily operations so we could grow our family and she could stay home. She was now going to take over the leadership role on-site.

The decision became official in February, and Rebecca began making overnight trips back to Port Orchard to ease herself into

Rebecca (three months pregnant) and me on the opening day of our coffee shop YES Please! Coffee. Port Orchard, Washington. 2004. *Raney Family Collection*

the role. I stayed in Glacier and assumed my new role as stay-at-home dad. Neither of us was excited about this role reversal, but we did it anyway. It was awesome being around Madrona all the time, but I didn't want to see my career disappear. I wanted to work.

During those times when Rebecca was gone, Madrona and I hitched rides with friends up the road to Mount Baker. Sometimes a friend would watch Madrona in the lodge so I could ride a few laps on the hill, and other times I would play with her on the rope tow. At the end of the day we would stand out in the parking lot with our thumbs pointed skyward and wait for a ride home.

February is an exciting time for Glacier, and more people were coming into town daily in preparation for the Legendary Banked Slalom. The race is the longest-running event in snowboard history, and I was getting excited. Many of the world's best snowboarders show up to compete in the race, and it is fun to watch them in person. One of those snowboarders is Tom Burt, who was driving up from Lake Tahoe that week for the event. Tom Burt is an icon in the world of snowboarding. He would later become like a brother to me and a constant source of encouragement to my family. At the time, I only knew Tom as an acquaintance through our mutual friend Temple Cummins. As far back as anyone can remember, Tom had been coming to Mount Baker and competing in the Legendary Banked Slalom. In previous years I had the good fortune of being entered in the race as well, and so I would see Tom in the wax area at Temple's condo. I wouldn't talk much as we all tuned up our boards, but I listened in awe while Tom told stories. He has a vast expanse of mountain knowledge and a ton of experience to share, but it was always his electric charisma and unyielding positive energy that excited me the most.

I saw Tom the morning after he arrived. Approaching me at the rope tow where Becca and I played with Madrona, Tom skipped all formalities by simply saying, "I hear you have the sickness," and then laughed in his disarming way as he gave me a hug.

I laid out for him all that had happened over the last six months, starting at the beginning when I hit my head surfing. I rambled on for a while and completed my dismal update by admitting that within a few months I would probably be done with snowboarding forever. Adding a bit more to my pity party, I said, "I don't think I can show up to race. I have a spot, but I don't think I can do it." Tom just laughed some more and said, "Go get your board, and let's figure this out."

Almost intuitively, I began riding ten feet behind him and trying to mimic his every move as we worked to fine-tune the technique we soon began calling tandem snowboarding. At first, I simply tried to stay on him as close as possible so that I could catch his every movement. I also relied heavily on what my brain already knew from having fifteen years of snowboarding experience. Simply put, if I stayed directly behind Tom, I knew that I wouldn't crash into anything—unless Tom stopped abruptly, and then all I would hit would be him.

On the chairlift after each lap, we discussed how my peripheral vision worked and then how to use the remaining 15 percent of my eyesight in a way that would allow me to follow him closer, tighter in the turns, and faster down the hill. Tom is a teacher, a problem solver, and a talker. He can talk a problem through for so long that a solution eventually just appears.

"What do you see, Raney?" Tom asked, with a heavy emphasis on the word "do." "Don't tell me what you don't see, Raney. Just tell me what you do see and we will use what's left." He wanted to know what worked; he didn't care about what was gone or broken. He and I are similar in this way. I loved hearing him say that. It reminded me of times on the job site when I would say, "Don't tell me what we can't do; just tell me what we can do."

I smiled. "Alright, Burt," I said. "I can see colors ... sort of." He laughed, then asked what I meant. "I mean, I don't like using the word 'see' because it's not the same as it is for you. When I say I can see colors, I mean I can see a difference in colors as they present themselves to me against different backdrops. They are never very clear, and it really depends on the contrast whether or not I can identify a clean separation between colors or objects."

"Oh my God, Raney. Give it to me simple. Can you see the color of my jacket?" Tom laughed. I looked over at him as we rode the chairlift and moved my eyes in circles as I tried to use my sideways vision to pick up the contrasting colors.

"It's beige," I stated proudly. "I can see the contrast at your cuffs where your black gloves punch through."

"Nice," Burt replied.

"Yeah, but that jacket doesn't show up very strongly against the snow when we're cruising," I said.

"OK," Tom said enthusiastically. "Tomorrow I'll wear a black one."

Tom then noted that it was in my favor that snow is white. He asked if I could see the tree line. I told him I could, and it came in handy on overcast days, when the clouds turn the snow and sky the same gray, giving me vertigo. "I can't tell up from down," I explained. "We get a lot of gray days here at Baker, and on those days I try to ride near the trees as much as possible so I get some depth perception and definition in the sky."

"That happens to me too," Tom said, and I agreed that I had experienced the sensation in whiteout conditions before my vision loss.

"When you see things out of the sides of your eyes, is it clear or is it blurry?" he asked.

"I don't know," I replied sheepishly. "It's pixelated, like the way old digital cameras would show things that were out of focus. It's not necessarily blurry—and it doesn't make me seasick—it's just slightly fuzzy and without definition." Tom asked if the center portion of my field of vision was black. "No, it's a giant gray smudge, like an eraser smudge or dark thundercloud."

"What happens when I put my finger in front of your goggles?" Tom asked, and I knew he was probably holding a finger right in front of my face. When I told him I could only see the smudge, he asked, "What if I move it over here?"

"I pick up the movement first, and if it's close enough I can tell it's a finger, but probably because I've known what a hand is for thirty-three years. The eye doctor says my eyesight is classified as having the ability to count fingers at a foot."

"Crazy," he said. For the rest of the day Tom would regularly yell, "Raney, just don't hit anything dark!"

The following day Tom wore a black jacket, and it was amazing how much easier it was for me to follow him by the definition black on white provided. I told him that the more he moved, the easier it was for me to see him. After I suggested that he look for tight sections, ride up the walls, and cut back across, he responded, "Sweet, I like gullies."

In the open runs Tom would carve more turns than usual and wave his arms to give me additional motion indicators to follow. He also shouted verbal cues, but we realized our speed was too fast for my brain to catch up before I ran over whatever it was that made him shout in the first place.

At the end of that first day, I felt like I had been led around the mountain by a rope. My neck was sore from tracking Tom's every move. Eventually my neck muscles would adjust and the new muscles I was using would grow stronger. We left our boards outside the White Salmon Lodge and went in to find Rebecca and Madrona, and we all headed for the parking lot.

"Will I see you tonight at Temple's for the wax party?" Tom asked.

"Oh yeah, Burt. I'll be there putting on the good stuff. If there's one thing I need right now it's more speed," I said sarcastically.

"That's the spirit, Raney," he said, grinning and nodding his head. "We get our first runs tomorrow. You're showing up, right?"

I smiled. "I always show up, Burt. You know that."

As we all walked on, I started to get lost in my head, thinking back to the day when I had learned one of the most valuable lessons of my life.

In the sixth grade, I was small, lean and bony, mouthy, and slightly handsome. The girls liked me. I was the perfect target for the bigger, more developed and frustrated boys. I also liked to mix it up, doing my share of recess trash talk, but I always respected the rules of playground justice. This code maintained natural order with short accounts and swift punishment. Thirty years later, I don't know of a better system. All matters were settled by the last bell. It was rare, but if things couldn't be worked out at recess, then an after-school fight was scheduled.

Most of the time on the playground, things ended in wrestling matches, which, at their worst, provided bloody knees and grass-stained elbows. The cuts and bruises were fine, but I hated the Chinese Tickle Torture.

This medieval technique was when someone would pin me to the ground face up while he used his knees to hold my shoulder blades down. As soon as I was pinned, he banged fast and hard on my chest bone with his index finger. The Chinese Tickle Torture was finished after the sadist aimed a long stream of spit into my mouth, which was wide open from the yelling I was doing. He usually hit his mark.

I was rarely sick as a kid. Writing this, years later, makes me wonder if my adolescent immune system had built up superhuman antibodies as a result of having my mouth spat in on a regular basis.

During the first recess on a Friday, a kid in my class named Jeff came up to me and said, "Tim wants to fight you at three o'clock."

"Why?" I asked.

"He says you're a pussy."

Those were fighting words, and I firmly retorted, "Fine."

Tim was on my soccer team. We had separate recess times and even though all of sixth grade had the same lunch hour, I hardly ever saw Tim, and we never spoke at school.

I sat in third period wondering what had set Tim off and why he had called me a pussy. I didn't think about it for long. Who cares? I thought. He's the one throwing down the challenge. Then the bell rang and I went out for second recess.

On the playground in sixth grade, wearing Vans skate shoes. Valencia, California. 1987.
Raney Family Collection

Word had spread fast, and I got the feeling kids were planning their Friday night around our fight. My school let out just after two and our fight was scheduled for three. More than a few kids came up to me, saying, "You're gonna show, right? Because I don't want to waste my time coming back to school grounds if you're scared."

Some kids walked up and told me straight up, "I don't think you're going to win." Popular opinion in the yard favored a quick victory by the challenger.

My two buddies just stood silently by. Although I was grateful they weren't giving me false hope, I did need some basic support. Turning to my friend Matt, I said, "What's the deal?" Looking stoic, he shrugged. "Tim is a lot bigger than you. But you're faster." Nodding, I pretended to know what he meant. The bell rang and I brooded over it until lunch.

A scheduled fight was familiar to me, as I had watched other fights as far back as fourth grade. Attendance was usually high. The more spectators, the bigger the circle, the arena, got. *The arena was needed to keep a fighter with cold feet from taking off.*

The scheduling idea was simple, and the three o'clock start was tradition. Since the fights took place on the grass field in the back corner of school property, we knew that teachers had a right to break them up. So the fights were always scheduled at three on Fridays after teachers had left for the weekend. Every kid knew that teachers went home early on Fridays.

I began second-guessing my strengths, which was causing me to reduce my own odds. I wished I could just fight Tim at lunch. If this self-doubt continued, I was not going to show up after all. Thoughts of quitting before the battle even started were making me nervous.

Lunchtime came with the bell. I was anxious about going into the yard. Would I see Tim? Maybe he would just come over for a talk and say, "Hey man, I was wrong. You're not a pussy, but the coolest dude at school." Probably not, I figured, but I didn't give up hope.

It wasn't Tim who came to see me, but one of his buddies. He seemed mad, and said, "Tim heard you weren't showing." Wondering if these guys had some sort of psychic powers, I said, "Oh, no. He's wrong. I'll be there."

Everything being said in the yard about Tim's size and strength was true. I knew it because I played soccer with him. Still, why had no one asked me what I thought my chances were? I did not like the fact that I was allowing popular yard opinion to affect the way I saw myself.

I did get a nice offer from a kid I barely knew. His parents and mine were in some club together. His name was Danny, and he approached me at lunch, saying, "My mom can give you a ride and you can come with me to my piano lesson." But I was disgusted, and responded appropriately. "What! Why would I do that? I have a bike, and I'm fighting at three." I walked away hoping someone on the yard heard me yell at him.

After lunch, I began believing what most of the school already seemed to know. Tim was going to win this fight. This was my first experience with self-doubt of this magnitude. I had often second-guessed myself, but at that moment, I didn't believe in my abilities. I was totally aware that if I didn't show up at three and fight Tim, I would go the rest of my life not showing up. It was simply a fact, and no teacher, school counselor, or psychologist could've gotten the message across better. I said to myself, *If you give up now, you will give up every time.*

This realization steeled my resolve, and when the bell sounded, I knew what I would do. Riding my bike home, I worked out how I was going to tell my mom. I would need to leave my house quickly, because it took me ten minutes to bike back to school. There was no wiggle room for debate with my mom if I was going to be on time to get my ass kicked. The only option was to just walk in and hit her with the truth. Hopefully she would respect what I had to do. If she did not, and ordered me to stay home, I was prepared to walk out and take the punishment later.

Blowing through the front door, I found my mom in the kitchen and, skipping hello, jumped right into the day's events. I finished by telling her what Tim had called me. With little emotion, she said, "Wow, that is not a nice word." Trying hard to be resolute, I replied, "No, it's not."

Moving toward the refrigerator, she said frankly, "You need to eat something before you go." I sat down, aware of the time, and had a snack courtesy of my supportive mother. When I was leaving, the only thing she said was, "Be home for dinner." It would be many years before I realized how big a gift it was that she let me fight my battles on my own.

I left in a rush, and I wondered if anyone making up the circle of spectators would be there to cheer for me. Seconds later, I saw my buddy Matt biking out from his street to join up with me. He shouted, "We gotta stop by David's too! He's waiting for us."

The three of us pedaled onto school grounds and approached the crowd. I saw Tim; he had gotten there before me, and his buddies had already started to heckle me. This was not the start I wanted, but I knew it would go fast now. The fear was gone. I had been afraid of the failure that would come from not showing up, and that battle was over. The physical act of fighting didn't bother me too much. There was never a clear winner, and I knew we would both get hurt somehow.

Tim advanced as I got off my bike. The mob followed and the circle formed around us. I heard Matt yell to me, "Don't worry, no one will jump in!" Then I heard some more yelling, mostly, "Get him, Tim!" and "Do it, Tim!"

We both stood there, and I wondered if he would do the thing he came for.

Seconds later, he made good on his promise and punched me in the eye. I took it, and followed it up with more speed than he was ready *for. Hitting Tim's ear, and then wrestling him to the ground, I found myself on top of him.*

I sat on his chest using the Chinese Tickle Torture almost involuntarily. With his shoulders pinned, I was ready to begin pounding his face. I guess he saw the beating coming because he started screaming, and then someone pulled me off him.

The circle opened up to let me out, and Matt and David walked away with me, unable to hide their pride as we went. "You won, you kicked his ass," they kept saying.

The lesson I learned that day always stuck with me—but so did the feelings of uncertainty, fear, and doubt. However, although there would be a lot of failures over the next thirty years, none of them would be a result of not showing up.

The next morning, I met up with Tom, and as we loaded the chair he said to me, "I'm going to ride high on the bank when we do our heel-side turns." I could tell he had been thinking about our upcoming run all night. "You stay lower on those heel-side banked turns, and I think I can look over my shoulder and watch how you're doing. We're stronger and more fluid when we do our toe-side turns, so follow me tight on those. It's easy to see back uphill on my toes, so I shouldn't have a problem watching you even if we're hauling ass."

In the afternoon we lurked around the staging area at the top of the course. "My legs are getting stiff, Burt," I said. "Maybe we should go for a hike and skip it."

"Quit whining, Raney. You're up soon." I buckled my binders and when my name was called, I wiggled into the start shack. Tom was in front of me, the nose of my board lapping over the tail of his, and he positioned himself so that he was just outside the timing wand. My time would start at the moment I pulled past the wand and not when he started. "Let me know when you're ready, Raney!" he shouted.

Although "ready" seemed like an overstatement, I nervously shouted back, "Let's go on three!" I counted down, Tom dropped into the track below me, and I pulled out of the shack as he went into the first banked turn.

Opposite: Tom and me in sync at the 2016 Legendary Banked Slalom. It has been a pleasure to follow Tom Burt for over a decade. Mount Baker, Washington. *Kevin McHugh*

I followed Tom through every banked turn and fell only once. The physical act of railing through the banked turns wasn't as much fun as it used to be, and I didn't manage to qualify for the final, but I felt a stronger sense of accomplishment when I crossed the finish line than I ever had before. I truly had to let my mind go and trust him. It was still exhilarating, but there was a tense feeling that hadn't been there before. I hoped over time that feeling would subside.

On Saturday, I showed up for my second chance at qualifying for Sunday's final. Tom and I repeated our run and I fell in the same turn as the day before. I could hear people yelling and hooting for us the entire way down, and I was having fun.

Tom was racing in the finals on Sunday. His group, the Pro Masters, was the next fastest category behind Pro Men. He took his runs in the morning, and we all stood at the rope line and yelled for him. Afterward he came and found me. "Let's go, Raney," he said. I grabbed my board and asked what we were doing. "Going up to the course for your runs," he answered matter-of-factly. When I reminded him that I didn't qualify, he explained that he had spoken with Gwynn Howatt, the general manager at Mount Baker, and she had agreed I could have two runs in the final. Although I protested his pulling those strings for me, I was excited. We took the two runs. I fell in different turns this time, but people were stoked and I felt good.

In the late afternoon the awards ceremony was held inside the White Salmon Lodge. Rebecca had gone inside early to hold a table. I stayed out on the hill and rode fun laps behind Tom. When the chairlifts shut down, we made our way inside. I sat listening to Gwynn call out the names of each category's top finishers and silently hoped to hear the names of my friends.

Then Gwynn said, "We want to give this next award to a guy who is losing his sight to a genetic disorder. You may have seen Tom Burt leading a snowboarder down the course, and that rider is Devon Raney. Where are you, Devon? Come down here and get this jacket!"

I went down to the staging area, gave Gwynn a hug, and accepted the award. My eyes started to well up and I was super grateful for all the positive energy. For a brief moment, I felt normal and capable again. Then when I started to walk back to our table and tripped over somebody's foot, the reality of my eyes came back to me.

On Monday morning, Tom stopped by our cabin before he left for Tahoe. We rehashed a few of the rad moments from the previous days. Then Tom said, "Alright, Raney, keep your chin up. You're probably going to have to figure out a new way to do most everything."

"Yeah, I know," I replied. "I am starting to think it's possible, though. I had a great time, Burt."

"Me too. I'll talk at you later." On his way out the door, he hugged Rebecca and said, "You're probably gonna have to learn a few new things yourself."

Rebecca closed the door, and we went to sit next to the fire. "You know," I said, "Tom is the perfect example of the responsible rebel. He has a defiant spirit and lives life on his terms and does it in a rad way. He takes care of his family, figures stuff out, and isn't worried about what others think of him. I hope I'm like that when I'm in my forties."

"You know, some of my early rebellious role models were not good examples," I added, laughing.

"Oh yeah, like who?" she asked. Rebecca sounded interested, so I recounted a story about my early days.

I spent all of my time outdoors as a kid. This was a gift from my mother, who, during the summertime, didn't let me back inside while the sun was out. Early in the summer of 1987, before my seventh-grade year, I became the proud owner of a vintage motor scooter. I acquired it the way I got most things during that time: it fell into my lap, and I went with it.

At the entrance to our neighborhood was a steep hill. I lived in the town of Valencia, California, and on days without much action, I would walk up the steep road to the top and then head toward the water tower. I'd jump a chain-link fence to access the fire roads and then cruise the dry hills full of sagebrush and look for adventure.

I always had to pass Jason's house on my way. I don't think I ever learned Jason's last name, and up till that point we had never exchanged a word. Jason had a white Chevy Camaro, with a T-top. It was a late-seventies model, but at the time it seemed brand new. Probably because he was always washing and babying it.

My brother Blake (left) and me (second from left) with two early neighborhood buddies—there has always been a crew. Yosemite, California. 1987.
Raney Family Collection

Jason had smooth, long black hair, down past his shoulders in the back but cut short on the sides and front. I learned later this was called a "mullet," but back then I just thought it was lame. I put him at around twenty years old, but I soon found out he was heading into his senior year of high school. "If I go back at all," he told me.

Jason always wore band T-shirts, black ones, which he said he got at the concert he just went to. My buddies and I knew he was lying. He always had the exact T-shirt our local music store displayed on a hanger right above the cash register. Every time they put up a new heavy metal shirt in black, Jason would be wearing it a week later. When he was out washing that Camaro, my friends and I would yell from across the street: "How was that Metallica show?" Followed by, "All time right, dude?"

But that was later, when we were older and after we had learned how big of a fraud he really was. This summer we still thought Jason was some outlaw legend, always going to shows, never sleeping, and fixing up his hot rod. The one thing he did well, after a high school career spent in auto shop, was wrenching on his car. Without fail, when I would walk by, the hood would be up and Iron Maiden would be blowing speakers in the garage.

It was no surprise that on this day the scene was the same. I could hear the Maiden before I could see the car. While I was walking past his driveway, Jason spoke to me for the first time, but I didn't hear him.

"What?" I asked.

He got mad, puffed up a bit, and said it again all tough-guy style. "You wanna buy a scooter?"

Hell, yeah, I thought. But all I said was, "Where is it?"

"It's in my garage," he said. "Come here—I'll show it to you."

For a brief second I thought he might jump me, but the risk seemed worth it as I realized this might be a one-time offer. Besides, ever since I was a small child I have harbored an inner belief that I could hold my own against anyone. So, overconfident in my skills as a seventh-grade scrapper, I followed Jason to the back of his garage.

I was surprised when he actually had a scooter. It looked rad to me, and instantly I could see myself the talk of all my bros. They would be on bikes, and I could hear them in my head: "Dev, let me try the scooter, man."

Still, reality set in. No matter what he was asking for the two-wheeler, I was sure it was more than I had. But I asked anyway.

"Sixty bucks," he replied.

I didn't think I heard him correctly. "What?" I said.

He got all tough-guy again, which I quickly learned was his reaction anytime he had to repeat himself.

Harshly, he said, "Sixty bucks if you go get the money right now."

I tried to stay chill, but I bet he saw it in my eyes, and I am sure he heard it in my voice.

"I'm coming right back."

Running to my house, I thought of where I was going to find the money. I briefly considered calling my buddy Travis and sharing the good fortune by splitting the cost. I quickly abandoned the idea when I realized I would have to split ownership as well—half the summer in his garage.

Hell no, I thought.

After tearing my room apart I found forty dollars, ten of which was in change. I did not see Jason objecting; there seemed to be some urgency in his sales pitch. I would need to borrow twenty from my younger brother, Blake. And by promising to pay it back, I would avoid any claim he might feel in regard to ownership. I could avoid this heated discussion altogether if I simply borrowed the money without letting Blake know, and made a personal promise to myself to put it back later.

My brother had not yet learned to lock up his allowance, or even hide it, and we all knew it was in a cigar box on his dresser shelf. Over the next few years I would do my job as older brother to teach him a valuable life lesson: he needed to get a lockable box. So I permanently borrowed the cash and went back up the street to seal the deal.

Jason didn't talk much—he just wanted the thing gone, quick. Still, I knew better than to pay him without seeing him start it first. I tried to be cool as I slowly walked around the scooter trying to identify something I could name as part of my buyer's inspection. I felt the tires for pressure, and while doing so I noticed the air valves looked to be the same kind I had on my bicycle. Now I was really stoked, as I already owned a bike pump.

Jason fired up the mighty motor; it started up on the first kick and blew white smoke out the muffler in a huge cloud. Before long the whole garage was full of smoke. I wondered if that was normal, but Jason didn't say a word. He did, however, seem to like the smoke.

I was ready to go and didn't want to shut off the motor. I had the panicked feeling that if the motor died, the dream died with it.

So I said, "Thank you."

"Oh yeah, it doesn't have a title," Jason said.

"Don't worry about it," I quickly replied, "I will give it a title," and rode out the garage and down the hill.

Gussy was the name of a pack mule I had memories of, and blue was the color of my newly purchased iron horse, so it became Blue Gussy. All my buddies loved the name, and in those days, no nickname stuck unless the whole crew validated it. The name Blue Gussy held, and that entire summer she proved to be the single greatest return on sixty bucks I had ever made. Although to be honest, I hadn't invested sixty dollars in anything at that point in my life, so the magnitude of the purchase was its own reward.

My parents seemed unconcerned about the deal, even to the point of not asking how I paid for it. My dad knew it would only take up slightly more room in an already-packed garage, and more kids would be coming around to check out Gussy, so he turned a blind eye.

My mom was the big surprise. I didn't expect her to ask much about the scooter, but I was confident she would track down the source of the money. It is possible that given the vintage look of Blue Gussy, she may have assumed I got her for free. I think she left me alone because she was busy with three kids and my own motor scooter meant fewer trips in the car for her.

Independence for me and my friends came at an early age. A bicycle allowed us to get to know our environment with the intimate knowledge of a farmer who tends his fields. I could make it to the grocery store faster than my mom could get there in her car because I knew every shortcut, backyard goat trail, and side alley in town. I don't think our parents ever realized that we could be seven or eight miles away in an hour. I generally got the feeling that all of our parents assumed we were out biking in the neighborhood. Which, of course, was the only place we were not.

Blue Gussy had just made my world a whole lot bigger. Or so I dreamed. I was fairly sure she was not legal on freeways, but as far as I was concerned, everything else was fair game.

Given that there was no Internet then, if I were going to check on the age requirement to ride the scooter I would have to actually call the police department. I figured I would also have to make a visit for some paperwork or something. This was an absolute no for me. As far as my friends and I were concerned, the only way we would visit a police station was in handcuffs.

I made a general inquiry, however, by calling a few older surfers I looked up to, who always seemed like they knew stuff.

One of them said, "Scooters with pedals are just like bikes. Does yours have pedals?"

"No," I said.

"Bummer."

Another guy I contacted said he knew the answer. "How many cc's is the motor?" he inquired.

"Fifty," I replied.

"Oh yeah, you're good, man," he said, and that was the end of any concern I had about road rules.

What little care I had for the law turned out to be a moot point anyway. For mechanical reasons, Blue Gussy didn't have the power I'd hoped for. To climb the steep hill of our neighborhood, I would have to *run alongside her while holding the throttle open full bore. Once I got to a level street, I would jump on and Gussy would top out at around twenty miles per hour. Still, this was not a disappointment to me, since it was a lot faster than I pedaled my bike.*

We also spent a fair amount of time researching ways that a 50 cc motor could be boosted. Hoping for a modified exhaust pipe, or a bored carb, we dreamed big. However, we tended to have no money, and so focused on easy solutions like octane booster, or a more scientific tire pressure ratio that we hoped would seriously increase speed.

Also, the blue smoke out the exhaust seemed to be increasing in output. One of my friends said it was burning automatic transmission fluid, so I began carrying a quart of ATF with me at all times. This became a constant source of chiding from my friends. That following year at junior high, people I didn't even know would walk by and say, "How are those ATF levels, man?" and then laugh. But I didn't care; their moms dropped them off, and I had a vintage scooter locked up at the bike rack.

Blue Gussy may not have met the specific expectations I had in my head, but she provided plenty of fun and a full day's adventure. Gussy and I ended up mostly limited to sidewalk travel, but at twenty miles per hour we tore those sidewalks up. I still ended up going farther across town by myself than I had on my bike. I would get off Gussy at crosswalks, run alongside her, and hit the sidewalk on the other side. But it turned out I didn't like "across town" that much, and all my friends lived closer to home anyway.

Jason, the wannabe tough guy who sold me Blue Gussy, was a poser. In stark contrast, Eric was the real deal. Although we were in the same grade and were the same age, Eric possessed a worldliness akin to someone in his late twenties. As a seventh-grader, he was already cynical, angry, and bitter.

Eric was a stoner, a hesher through and through. There was only one other person whose status as a hesher was more elevated than Eric's, and that was Chad. Chad had been kicked out of the school district for repeatedly wearing his favorite Metallica T-shirt that displayed the following graphic: a toilet and an arm rising out of the bowl with the hand gripping a knife pointed straight up; the caption read, "Metal up your ass."

I was there in class when he refused to take it off and was escorted away by security, whom Chad called a "rent-a-cop." I was in awe, thinking he was a hero with brass balls who stuck to his principles. Chad's going places, *I thought. It turned out that he wasn't going back to school.*

If stoners and heshers had an order of command, Chad would have been the general and Eric the colonel. It was rumored that Eric was dropping out of school so Chad could have someone to bike around town with during the day. But I kept seeing Eric in class, so I figured it was talk. Eric had been shaving since I met him, which was in fifth grade. I also believe that was the year he took up smoking as well. But he didn't show us how to buy cigarettes until the fall of eighth grade.

My friends and I were going to try our hand at smoking, but we didn't know how to buy the cigs. A kid at school said he could steal some from his mom and promised to sell us a few, but every day he said he forgot. We were getting tired of his excuses and I had the uneasy feeling we were going to need Eric's help, which in general meant something else was going to happen, usually something bad.

My friends and I didn't want Eric to think we couldn't handle ourselves, and so we asked him for info in some dumb roundabout way, saying things like, "Where did you get your Marlboros, man? I get mine from my uncle."

But Eric was a man of the world and saw right through our bullshit. I finally got him to agree to take me with him next time he bought smokes, but only me. I passed on the news, and we waited. Some weeks later he came up to me and said, "Be at the bus stop an hour early tomorrow morning."

I didn't really want to go with him, but I was beginning to develop an approach to life that required me to see every opportunity as the chance to take a road less traveled. I was again convincing myself, "I probably won't get this chance twice."

So, no questions asked, I agreed.

Showing up early was not a problem. I simply told my mom I was going in for special tutoring, which in a way was true, because I learned a ton from Eric.

We met at the bus stop and began walking toward our local hotel, The Hampton Inn. I don't think Eric spoke once during the walk, and it felt just like I had seen big drug buys go down in movies: silent and serious. I assumed Eric knew someone who was eighteen and worked at the hotel. I wondered if I could get jail time for buying smokes underage. This led to another thought. Would I still be required to do my homework in prison? I weighed the pros and cons as we silently walked on.

Just as I was deciding that I would rather stay in school than go to prison, since there were no girls in prison, we entered the hotel. I followed Eric as he walked right up to a vending machine. Dumbfounded, I stared at the row of pull levers and then at all the packs of cigarettes. I said to myself, There's no way it's this easy.

Eric punched my shoulder. "You got the two-fifty I told you to bring?"

"Yes," I said and fished it out.

Handing it over, I instinctively knew what was happening. That was the price of today's lesson, and I wouldn't be getting any smokes of my own. Eric pulled some Marlboro Reds from the machine. I am pretty sure he picked the kind without filters. Thinking we were done and nervous, I was ready to leave. Eric had other plans, however, and I followed as he went toward the back exit.

We walked down one of the hotel hallways and found the housekeeper's cart. I watched as he promptly filled his pockets with the little bottles of mouthwash. Logically, I assumed the mouthwash was to hide the smoke smell; again, I was in awe of the things Eric knew. I was surprised, and then horrified, while on our way to school Eric drank the contents of two of the bottles.

"They get you buzzed," he said matter-of-factly.

It seemed like a pretty solid start to his day. I'd paid for his smokes and he was already working a mouthwash buzz.

I wasn't allowed to go to Eric's house. My mom didn't know the family, and she had not even met Eric. Some things a parent just knows, and one day while driving past his house my mom pointed and said, "Don't hang out there."

Ultimately, this is what led to the death of Blue Gussy. In secrecy, I rode her down to Eric's one afternoon and stayed too long. I was late for dinner, which wasn't tolerated during the school year. This tardiness most likely caused me to be in a rush when trying to start Gussy. She didn't cooperate, and it is possible through further attempts I flooded her, only making it worse.

Normally I would have waited, but I decided to run home this time and leave Blue Gussy at Eric's. This was the fatal mistake, and during dinner I realized it: Anything left at Eric's becomes Eric's.

I tried to come up with a solid scheme to get out of the house but couldn't.

The following afternoon, I went right down to Eric's house to pick up my scooter and stood in horror. She was leaning against his garage door, her entire body painted with flat black spray paint, and in red the names of death metal bands—Megadeath, Metallica, Slayer, and Maiden. Each looked like it had been written in fake blood all over what was once Blue Gussy. She looked hurt, weathered, and abused. She had been captured by heshers and I knew there was nothing I could do.

My mom was loose with things like adventure, and she never questioned me when I bought the scooter. But I knew there was no way in hell she would let me garage anything with Megadeath and Slayer painted in blood!

So I walked back home with the same feeling I had from watching the movie Old Yeller. *I never laid eyes on Blue Gussy again, and I was back on my bicycle the next day.*

Rebecca was laughing when I finished my story. "That sounds like you," she said.

"Yeah, well, when I heard Chad call that security guard a rent-a-cop, I mistook his disrespect for courage," I said as I started to laugh. "I just thought he had the courage to stand up for himself and I secretly questioned whether I could do the same. After high school, I got lucky and met a few guys like Tom who used their rebellious spirit in positive ways. I started looking up to people who found ways to get what they wanted from life while taking a less traditional path."

I was silent for a long time. "I've been hoping for months now that my defiant spirit will get me through being disabled," I confided in Rebecca.

"You know, when we first started hanging out, my mom used to tell me, 'He's a rebel, Honey. He's a rebel,'" Rebecca said. "She knew I wanted a rebel, and I got one."

"I just need to believe that rebel is still inside me somewhere and he's going to keep me from giving up."

I became proficient in the tandem technique Tom Burt and I had devised, and was able to ride with Rebecca, Madrona, or anyone else who was gracious enough to lead me to a powder stash. It was hard for people to recognize I had any form of vision impairment. Most folks just assumed I was following a buddy too closely. As a result, I tried not to expose my disability, believing that if a random person truly got the sense of how bad my vision was, they would ask Ski Patrol to remove me.

CHAPTER 6

Raised by Skaters and Surfers

We moved out of our Glacier condo rental on April 1, 2009, and moved back into our house.

Madrona turned four on April 16. The last visual memory I have of her beautiful face was when she was three-and-a-half years old. I tried not to think about this. It didn't do me any good. Instead, I tried to be as close to her as possible. Putting my nose to hers, I would use my peripheral vision to see whatever I could. I was constantly giving her Eskimo kisses. When I began to think about all the ways Madrona would change, how she would become a beautiful woman, and how I wouldn't be able to see any of this, it was simply more than my mind could take.

Madrona's four-year-old birthday party was held at the Gig Harbor skate park. She rode her bike around the bowls and skateboarded up the walls with one knee on the deck of her board, both hands on the nose of it, and pushing with her free leg for speed. We hung a piñata from the swing set in the park nearby and the kids took swings with a Wiffle ball bat. After a while I had to break apart the piñata by hand and throw the candy into the air. They all went crazy. It was a perfect party.

When the party was over, I took a few laps around the skate park on my own. I fell and smacked my face on the concrete. My cheek split open and started to bleed, and I could tell that swelling had begun below my eye socket.

About to take Madrona out for some gentle longboard waves. Campus Point, Goleta, California. Fall 2008. *Rebecca Raney*

Discouraged, I said it was time to go. Madrona took my hand and Rebecca drove us home.

Lying on the couch, I held the bag of ice against my cheek and closed my eyes in an effort to push away the headache beginning to set in. It was less than a year since I'd received my diagnosis. Although I had firmly accepted the fact that I would never drive again, I was still getting rides to the skate park and trying to find a way to keep skating. My only plan was to show up, keep trying, and believe a way to adapt would appear.

On my back, and fighting the headache, dark thoughts of despair and doubt began to cloud my mind. Feeling fragile, I said to myself, *Keep going, Devon. This is nothing like that time you couldn't move your legs.* Then I thought for a long time about the worst fall I had ever taken. Even after five years, my memory of the crash was vivid.

"Devon," she said, "do you know where you are?"

The woman had her hands in my mouth and was holding my tongue. She looked a bit panicked and I noticed a lot of commotion around me. The entire crew of teenage skateboarders was just staring. I tried to sit up, but my head was strapped down.

"Yes," I answered. "Seattle. At the skate park."

"Good," she said. "Do you know how old you are?"

I attempted to sit up and failed again. My whole body was secured to a stretcher. The paramedics moved around me and avoided eye contact.

"Can you wiggle your toes?" a paramedic asked.

"Yes," I said again, wondering how he expected to see my feet with my shoes still on. No reply. A moment later, someone walked by carrying my Vans.

"One ... two ... three." I felt the liftoff as I was transferred into an ambulance. Looking me in the eyes now, a medic said, "Can you feel this?"

"Feel what?" I asked.

"I'm poking you on your legs and feet."

"OK, do it," I responded. But he had already been poking for a while.

"What's wrong with my legs?" I asked.

"We don't know yet," he replied. "But you're looking good, buddy, real good."

He sounds just like my friends do when I get a bad haircut, I thought to myself. After a particularly bad haircut when I was a kid, my friend Travis had said the same thing in the same tone of voice. Realizing the paramedic was padding his optimism to candy-coat my situation terrified me even more.

Strapped down to a board, staring up at an ambulance ceiling, I began to cry. I tried to clear my throat before saying, "Can someone please call my wife? Also my brother, Blake—he lives close by." Silently, the tears rolled past my temples and pooled in my ears.

My ambulance arrived at 2 a.m. at Seattle's Harborview Medical Center, the top trauma center for the greater Pacific Northwest, where patients from as far away as Idaho are flown in by helicopter if their injuries are bad enough. As my stretcher burst through the double door leading into the emergency wing, the magnitude of my situation became real. This is bad, I realized, or I wouldn't be at the trauma center. Distracted by the flurry of ER activity surrounding me, my brain had not begun to spin off in thoughts about a life of paralysis.

As they transferred me from the stretcher into a hospital bed, I began to get a tingling sensation in my toes. Minutes later I had fully recovered my lower-body mobility and touch sensation. By the time Rebecca arrived, I was unstrapped and able to move my legs freely.

A CT scan revealed brain swelling, which was the cause of my temporary paralysis. The doctor kept me under observation until he was confident pressure would not need to be relieved by drilling a hole in my head. I acted like it was no big deal since I didn't want Rebecca to know how scared I really was, and because I was young and macho, or maybe just full of dreams for our future. Before he discharged me the doc said, "It's a good thing you were wearing a helmet, or you would be dead."

Still holding the ice pack against my face, I smiled the moment I recalled the doctor's words that day back in 2002. It gave me some hope, and I believed I would bounce back from the crash.

A month later I tried again, and was forced to accept the fact that I could not find a safe way to skateboard with only 15 percent of my vision left. There was not enough contrast between the gray concrete and metal coping edge of the bowls. I simply couldn't tell where the lip was. When I stayed in the flat bottoms and pushed through the park, I often hit a roller or concrete feature I couldn't identify because it just blended in with all the concrete around it. I was falling every time I tried to skate—and concrete is not forgiving.

I was thirty-four years old and could no longer continue skateboarding. The sport had been part of my life for more than twenty-three years. It had shaped me as a person in more ways than I might ever understand. The realization that I would be left with only memories from then on made me feel like a small part of myself was being shut off.

Skateboarding raised me, and I am grateful to have been brought up by skaters and surfers. Much of what I know about leadership, determination, and finding confidence in uncomfortable situations has evolved from those early experiences trying to prove myself.

I learned to skate transitions in a drainage ditch called Forevers. Built with rough concrete, it had been covered with layer upon layer of paint until the tiny porous holes were filled in and

Making perfect

SHAUN DYER/The Signal

A photo from our local newspaper of me skating the Forevers ditch. Valencia, California. Circa 1991. *Shaun Dyer/The Signal*

the surface became smooth. Skateboarders had done the work, and the paint was probably borrowed from random garages. The different colors used gave the place a tough, patchwork, vagrant appearance. Cement parking blocks were lined end-to-end along the top edge of the ditch to serve as coping.

During that time I also played soccer. I was never nervous about whether or not I belonged on the soccer team. Our parents had signed us all up and paid our fees, and I believe every player understood he had a right to be on the team.

In stark contrast, I would have to prove myself at the ditch. My parents certainly didn't sign me up for skate team. There was no coach, no one knew my name, and most skaters acted bothered when I arrived. I often confused the flow by dropping in before it was my turn, or before the present alpha ripper was going to let me have a turn. It was not a safe environment, but it was thrilling.

I would go to the ditch every day after school around 4 p.m. A few other beginners would show then as well, and all of us would try to get in as many runs as possible before 5 p.m. That was when the older guys arrived and took over. One of them would always leave a car door open, blast the stereo, and bring the energy up a few notches. I watched them surf the concrete walls, grind the parking curbs, and do "boneless airs" off the lip. Some guys had style, some did complicated tricks, and some just acted crazy. It was a colorful group and the only culture I wanted to be a part of.

It took courage to show up every day, but it took serious will-power to start dropping in while the older guys watched me. I remember that the first time I did, my knees were shaking, I was sweating, and I had the same weird sick feeling I got when my mom opened my report card. All those guys were staring at me as I dropped in, pumped the first wall, and then slammed in the flat bottom. I got up fast, ran back up to the top, stood with my board, and stared at my shoes. They all laughed and heckled me before they went back to skating.

Things went like that for a while. I left a lot of blood and skin on those concrete walls. Eventually the heckling turned to sarcasm and then took on a tone of acceptance. One evening, after the sun went down and the session ended, I was invited to go with the older guys and skate a half-pipe. Getting the invite to skate the ramp meant I had paid my dues and earned their respect.

It was a good feeling. It was also enlightening to realize that the respect I had earned came from my effort and consistency. I wasn't the best, the craziest, or the coolest. I just showed up every day, kept my mouth shut, and tried again after every slam. I gained a lot of confidence by going on my own and earning a place among that group of skaters.

It was hard to get excited about playing soccer after I began skateboarding. When I was with the team, I felt I had a deeper understanding of something the others didn't know about yet. I wasn't totally sure what that thing was, but the cozy boundaries of the soccer field didn't suit me anymore. I quit both soccer and baseball at the end of my freshman year of high school. For better or worse, I was skating and surfing from then on.

Paying dues, showing up consistently, and giving respect had been a part of surfing long before skateboarding came along. More to the point, those values are a part of any successful culture or person's life. I have just been lucky to learn these lessons while doing the things I love.

I was born in Goleta, California, a beach town just north of Santa Barbara. Sandy beaches, waves, and the way a sunburn stings after a saltwater ocean rinse are some of my earliest memories. I went surfing for the first time when I was nine in Ventura at the fabled point break known as C Street, just a few miles from my grandparents' house. I had already fallen in love with the beach and the water, but now I had been introduced to an activity that would stay with me for the rest of my life. Although it took a while for me to actually begin riding the wave out on the face in front of the whitewater, I was simply in awe of all things surfing. Soon I had my first board, a 4'11" IG Performance Thruster with 1980s neon paint splattered on the deck beneath a polished glass job.

Just before I turned ten, our family moved to Valencia. And although my area code was still 805, the same as Goleta and Ventura, we now lived inland, forty-five miles from the nearest beach. Fortunately, my grandparents on my dad's side still lived just three miles down the road from California Street in Ventura where they would remain for thirty more years. My cousins lived in Santa Barbara as well, and with some effort I would not lose my connection to my favorite beaches from Ventura on up to Goleta. I never passed up a ride, and later when I began driving, things improved significantly.

This move was a big change for my parents as well. My mom had grown up in Ventura, and gave the commencement speech when she graduated from Buena High. She met my dad at Westmont College in Santa Barbara. The two were married after graduation and hoped to stay around the area. Skyrocketing housing prices and high-interest mortgage loans made it almost impossible for young families to buy their own home during the mid-eighties. The trap of an affordable tract home couldn't be avoided, and we moved away from the beach into a stucco box with bedrooms for everyone, a two-car garage, and a pool.

Although I had a few friends who lived close enough to the ocean that they could bike to the beach, I did not know anyone who could actually see the waves from their house. So, I was taught by the older crew to read the swell report featured in our local newspaper.

This was during the late 1980s and the early 1990s, and before any surf report could be found with a Google search. Some guys were using weather radios, but the most effective way to check conditions was simply to go and look at the waves. Most of us knew to keep a handful of quarters around so we could use the beach pay phone to call a buddy at home if in fact the surf was good. At that point, whoever received the call would use their home phone to make a few more calls to other buddies, and eventually all of us would find our way to wherever the others were.

The golden rule "You have to go to know" is one of the most profound lessons I have learned about life in general. In many ways, that statement is the greatest gift Mother Nature and my passion for surfing have given me.

Surfing rounded out my worldview in a deep way. While many of the lessons I learned from skateboarding taught me the importance of overcoming fear in the moment, surfing taught me lessons about how to navigate through life on a daily basis.

Paddling is simple grunt work that is never finished. If you don't like to paddle, then quit surfing. I like to think of it as manual labor, like digging a ditch or using a push broom.

When I was young, I hated manual labor; it was hard. My grandpa used to say over and over, "If you learn to love hard work, you won't end up working a day in your life." He was right. Not long after I graduated high school, I forced myself to see manual labor as an awesome way to stay in shape. Since that time I have always loved construction, and part of that love comes from the tired feeling I get at the end of a day's work. It's an honest feeling, and I had to change my perspective to see that gift.

Riding wave faces and sitting in the pocket are the easy parts for me. The hard part has always been the work it takes in advance. This hard work is 80 percent of the sport, and becoming a familiar face in the lineup and moving through the pecking order takes work. At different times I have become a familiar face in a lineup. Then, after a while, I would start surfing somewhere else. After disappearing, I would return to the earlier spot and realize the hierarchy had shifted and new faces existed. If I wanted to become a familiar face again, I would need to start over. It was a good lesson: Life keeps moving on no matter what, and just because I did the hard work previously doesn't mean I am guaranteed anything. Starting over and doing it all again is a part of life. Every time I catch a wave, I am taking one away from someone else. Surfers don't give this up lightly. Understanding this pecking order made me aware of how I impact those around me in all situations. I learned my social graces in the water.

Understanding what conditions make different spots better than others also takes time, and should be done firsthand by every surfer, rather than researched on the Internet.

My biggest struggle with surfing is patience: Waiting on waves, going a little farther down the beach, and paddling out with the right tide can be rewarding efforts if a surfer is patient. I paddle out in waves if there is even a hint of swell. Surfing until I am exhausted, I have often gotten out only to watch from the beach as the conditions improve. *Whatever*, I tell myself. *I just had so much fun.*

The joy of riding perfect waves has only been given to me after I have done the hard work first. This has been the case for me in life as well; rewards, success, and achievement have all been the result of doing the hard work first. Surfing has taught me to look for the established order, watch how others do things, and remember that my presence, no matter how slight, is impacting those around me.

My value system developed over time. Work, consistency, and overcoming fear were part of my everyday process. The keystone, however, was the focus I put into earning things on my own and resisting the expectation that I would be given anything.

When I began my career in construction, I worked alongside rough and outspoken workers. The environment was much like the hierarchy I knew from skating and surfing. A pecking order existed, and any respect had to be earned. I did well doing what I learned through surfing and skating. I showed up every day, did the work, and kept my mouth shut until it was my turn to talk.

Later, as I moved into leadership positions that carried significant responsibilities, I would be given a title. As project manager I had the power to fire or hire. I knew from experience that my new

Opposite: This was a fun wave—the face went on forever. Baja, Mexico. 2018.
Colin Wiseman

title meant very little and I would now have to work harder in the field at earning respect.

I have seen many people carry a title in a way that implies they deserve respect because of their title. I feel fortunate to have spent my life around people who understand that the individual, not the title, earns the respect.

This lesson proved to be invaluable to me at the point when I realized I could no longer drive my truck, and ultimately no longer support my family as a home builder. During that time I would often say to myself, *The title doesn't make the man, Devon. The title doesn't make the man.*

Soon after Madrona's skate park birthday party, I signed up to coach basketball for three- and four-year-old kids at the YMCA. Fearful and uncertain of the future, I didn't want to go through life without having coached my kid at least once, so we put Madrona in recreational basketball. My friend Temple signed up his son, Cannon, too. With the hoops lowered to six feet, the basketballs mini-sized, and the court reduced in length by half, I had the pleasure of being "Coach Devon." I couldn't tell any of the kids apart, and so I avoided the use of first names by saying stuff like, "Nice shot, Bud!" or, "Way to go, Sweetie!" Although I could not tell boys from girls either, so even this was a bit of a gamble. I brought a whistle and a clipboard, formed layup lines, and then ran drills. Laughing all the time, I would yell, "Learn the fundamentals, kids, remember the fundamentals!"

At most practices I met some parents. I worked hard to hide my vision impairment and I tried to center my eyes on their faces despite losing them in my blind spot. We would go through general formalities, comment on the kids seeming like they were having fun, and at some point during the conversation I would get hit with the question, "So Devon, what do you do for work?"

"I am a builder," I would say.

"Oh, that's great. Do you have anything going right now?"

"No, not at the moment," would be all I could say.

My mind would race and I would doubt myself. Can I still be a builder? A growing sense of insecurity began to nag at me as I wondered if I would work again. All I could do was constantly remind myself, *The title doesn't make the man, Devon. The title doesn't make the man.*

During that first year, it was the loss of my driver's license and saying good-bye to a lifelong passion that hurt the most. I was putting my face up to Madrona's, holding Rebecca's body in my arms, and slowly finding ways to adapt or cope with everything else, but losing my license crushed my independence and the inability to skate shook my identity. Skateboarding and all it encompassed had played a big part in shaping my character, and I tried to be full of gratitude for what I had gained from the sport as I let the physical aspect of it go.

I was not, however, willing to let surfing go, and soon I would spend all my energy finding new ways to get to the beach and stay in the water.

CHAPTER 7

Go to Know

On a sunny day in June 2009, I took Madrona to the zoo with some friends who were up from California. It was a beautiful day, and my four-year-old took me to every exhibit. She loved the beluga whales, and we made two passes by their tank. Her favorite was the tiger, though, and she stood for over an hour just staring at the animal through the thick glass.

I didn't get it; the tiger was beautiful, no doubt, but it hardly ever moved. So sedentary was its behavior that any time the cat stood up to urinate or simply turn in a circle, an audible gasp was heard by loving viewers. It was a challenge for my short attention span—and dull eyesight—to stand at that glass for as long as Madrona could. Like many other dads, I did it anyway.

Madrona stood with her face glued to the glass, patiently waiting, and I stood with my hands in my pockets. After a while I realized our California friends were not standing next to us anymore. Out of habit I looked around, but since I was not able to recognize a face, it did no good. I told Madrona to stay put and went to walk around the viewing platform in hopes they might spot me. After a minute or two, I returned to where I had left Madrona. I let her stare for a minute longer and then decided we should go outside to the main path to look for our friends. Reaching down, I took her hand and said, "Let's go, Honey. We need to find our friends."

Madrona and the tiger. Point Defiance Zoo, Tacoma, Washington. 2009.
Raney Family Collection

We had gone about twenty feet and were near the exit when I heard a woman screaming, "That's my child, that's my child!" Seconds later, I realized she was yelling at me as she frantically pulled Madrona away from my hand. Only it was not Madrona. It was her daughter, and I was casually walking out of the tiger exhibit with her kid in tow.

I felt sick and apologized immediately, "I am so sorry. I have very bad eyesight. I am so sorry. My daughter is here too, somewhere, I promise. I am so sorry."

The woman did not respond, but she grabbed her kid fast and left in a hurry. It was quiet, and I could feel people staring at me. My chest was tight, and I was angry. Madrona came to me and took my hand, happy to see me. I gripped her hand tightly as we walked away.

It took only a few minutes before my anger faded. In its place was an emptiness I had never experienced. It was defeat, but not the simple feeling of defeat I had known many times—the defeat one experiences from a loss of a game or race, or of a goal one fails to meet. What I had always known of defeat was only temporary, a simple setback. My entire life I'd been able to push defeat away with hope and the resolve to try again. On that day I saw the face of permanent defeat. The feeling was suffocating. In a complete way, I knew I was fucked.

It was only a week before I did it again. While pretending to see the menu at Seattle's Ivar's fish stand, I confidently ordered some fish and chips for myself and Madrona. Turning and looking for a table, I took the arm of the girl beside me—and she was not Madrona. It was just a second before her attentive father stepped in. He was on edge. I was confused. It was awkward. Luckily I had a friend there who explained my mistake.

I had no tools to fight the rage, and no prevention plan for what I soon learned was the slow killer: bitterness. I was unwilling to use a cane or a guide dog; I didn't want to bring attention to my eyes. Staying away from crowds or social situations was not an option. How would my family deal with a life in seclusion? The only choice I felt I had was the same one I'd always made. I would show up, no matter what, and try again.

As a surfer, I learned to check the surf conditions by going to my beach and seeing for myself. This was wisdom passed down from the generation of surfers who had come before me. It was common practice for the older crew to remind everyone, "Go to know"—that we shouldn't solely rely on any weather report. By the time I was a young adult, I had developed an understanding of the weather patterns that created the best waves at my favorite beaches. Additionally, I'd learned what cycles had a negative effect on the surf, and I could spot a storm brewing before it hit the beach. Physically showing up to check the conditions was the best way to learn anything.

After that miserable day at the zoo, I experienced many more uncomfortable moments, but none of them hurt quite as bad. I would stumble off curbs, enter the women's restroom, and continually say "hello" to walkers talking on their cell phones or joggers with earbuds in. At the grocery store, cashiers would often refuse to help me swipe my bank card because they didn't think I looked blind. I understood their confusion because my eyeballs provided no obvious indication, but the challenge to "prove it" was getting old.

While I was working to relearn all the basics, I was also trying to keep engaged in Madrona's world. Parents of Madrona's friends would regularly offer to pick her up so she could have the playdate at their house. I would decline the ride and instead walk her over to the playdate. Then I would come back at pickup time so the two of us could walk home. I did not want to lose what bits of independence I had left.

Over time, as I became more confident in my role as a visually impaired dad, I began to insist that Madrona also hang out at our house with her friends, and I worked hard getting to know all of them. Those moments were a good opportunity to discuss my eyes, and I made jokes about how blind I was as a way of moving into the main thing I wanted them to know. I would say, "I can't see your faces, so remember to tell me your name. But don't worry: I can figure everything else out, so we can have lots of fun."

I would take Madrona and her friends on Puget Sound beach walks and look for shells. Sometimes I would get them started on an art project. We used stencils to spray-paint salmon on a sheet of plywood, and I taught them how to use my jigsaw to cut their fish out. Holding a life-size wooden salmon they had made using a power tool did wonders to keep their attention. Soon, the group was coming over all the time.

Rebecca and I began listening to TED Talks. One in particular resonated with me. Brené Brown gave a talk titled "The Power of Vulnerability." She said, "Vulnerability is the birthplace of creativity." Her words hit me like a slap in the face. Not only did I understand her statement to be absolutely true, but I recognized an absence of vulnerability in myself as well.

I had witnessed it before in people with big egos. I have watched some of those egos mentally block a person from being vulnerable, and therefore unable to be open to new ideas or be receptive to suggestions that aren't their own. When a person is blocked in this way, they cannot creatively see past their own issue.

Although I am not immune to having a swollen ego, that was not the issue blocking me from creative movement during that time. I was blocked by fear. I was scared of everything during that first year, but mostly I was scared of all the changes I needed to make if I was going to adapt. I was scared of failing and angry that I had to start all over after I had already put my life's energy into successfully building an amazing lifestyle for my family. I was afraid I lacked the strength to do it all again. Fear was blocking me from being vulnerable. I knew this at my core. I began to realize that if I didn't find a vulnerable place and find a way to ask for help, then I was going to fail as a result. It would be impossible to truly stay engaged with my family if I put up walls and then spent a lifetime hiding behind them.

So in July of the summer of 2009, I enrolled in a Mobility Training course offered by Lighthouse School for the Blind in Seattle. My younger sister, Laura, owned a house in the Magnolia district of town, and she graciously offered the three of us her entire first floor to live in Seattle during the three months of mobility instruction. Although I didn't enroll full time, there was a program available in which an instructor came to my location. We moved in and used Laura's house as the meeting point. Rebecca was stoked to hang with my sister for such a long stretch of time. We all were.

Mobility training was even harder than I had imagined, because it was a constant reminder of my new reality. The instructor spent the time teaching me all the techniques blind people use on a daily basis. Most were designed to create independence for the blind. Some of his instruction was focused on the ways a person's disability can be recognized at first glance, which he believed would make life easier. He said, "If a person can spot your disability instantly, then you will become more confident socially by avoiding any confusion from the get-go." I listened quietly.

He showed me the system blind people use to fold their cash. By folding each denomination in a different way, you can tell a twenty-dollar bill from a five. Eventually we got down to the real business and he showed me the tools. Since I like tools, I was excited to learn the ones I needed to be successful at being blind. First came the watch without a face. The wrist piece had a button instead and when I pushed it, a robot voice told me the time. "Pretty neat, right?" he said enthusiastically. "I guess," I responded dryly. Moving on, we examined a variety of hand-held binoculars and then a group of magnifiers for just one eye. These tools were intended for folks with vision better than mine as a way of seeing street signs from across the street. A few days later he showed me a type of closed-circuit television that magnified documents and photos—anything that fit in the fourteen-by-ten-inch tray below it. This was something I thought would be very useful, and I ended up getting my own a few months later. When I put my face to the screen, I could read three or four words at one time.

At some point during every lesson my mind would start to unravel, and all I could do was laugh at myself and how fast my world had flipped upside down. I had traded in my new Chevy truck to test-drive a strange-looking, donut-sized watch with a single button on its face meant to wake up a late-seventies robot who then shouted a number at me. If I couldn't laugh at that, I was in trouble.

In truth, my big fears could never be addressed by an instructor because there were no easy answers for the things that worried me the most. What I really wanted to ask was, "Do you think my daughter is going to be made fun of at school because I wear this watch, fold my money into origami, and use a cane?" I was trying to take the course seriously, but on many days I simply felt it didn't matter. Deep down, I was convinced that my eyes would at some point push everyone I cared about away from me. And who was going to train me to deal with that?

Finally, we began working on cane technique. I enjoyed this part of the class and truly saw how necessary the tool was for me at times. More than anything, it helped with recognition and significantly reduced the socially awkward interactions I had grown accustomed to every time I asked for assistance. "You don't look blind" had become the standard accusation. I began to use my new cane at the airport when I traveled by myself. Six years later, I would regularly use a juniper stick given to me by a friend. It had been crafted by his dad, and I started using it regularly after I took a few falls. I simply accepted the stick as an additional piece of fashion wear.

My final effort to become familiar with the ways blind people adapt came from Rebecca's wisdom. She remembered how Dr. Hamilton had stressed the importance of meeting others with the same diagnosis as mine. So Rebecca found an online forum dedicated to anyone dealing with Leber's hereditary optic neuropathy. Rebecca and I were introduced to new perspectives and we appreciated hearing from people who were in supporting roles.

Madrona on the porch of our 2009 Mount Baker cabin rental on a classic gray, drizzly Washington day. *Rebecca Raney*

A constant thread seemed to bind most people together, and that thread was found in the hope that technology and new medicine would improve things. It was suggested to me that I investigate an experimental vitamin available only in Canada, become proficient with the audio programs on my computer, and get to know the iPhone. These were all good ideas, but none of them got at what I really wanted to do. I wanted to play outside and continue chasing my passions.

In the fall we moved back into our house again. Our dream home had begun to feel like a temporary residence; I felt disconnected to the project I was once so proud to build. We enrolled Madrona in prekindergarten at an upscale private school called Gig Harbor Academy. We paid for the tuition using the line of credit on our house, which had been hemorrhaging money for almost two years. We wanted Madrona to have some form of stability during a time of upheaval. Rebecca and I were uncertain if we would be able to stay in our house and didn't know what school district we might land in. We avoided any enrollment boundaries by sending her to private school, and so we cut a check and dipped further into the red.

In December we found the cheapest Glacier snow cabin possible. It was just over 300 square feet and without insulation in the floors or walls. It had a woodstove, a couch, a two-burner range, and two lights. It cost us $350 a month, and we tried to show up for every storm at Baker to repeat the magic we felt every winter. I hooked up with Tom Burt at the Banked Slalom, and we had another fun week riding together and racing the course in tandem.

It had become painfully clear that Rebecca was our full-time taxi service, taking Madrona to playdates, kindergarten, and the YMCA. She took me to all the same places and then to the beach or the mountains depending on the season, and she took us all to the store when we needed something. I watched with heartache as she began to lose more independence than even I had. It was obvious to me that I needed to find us a new place to live. And through it all, the money bled out.

Toward the end of winter, Rebecca said, "We need to talk about money." I agreed and asked her when. "In the morning, after we drop Madrona off," was her swift reply.

It was not a discussion. Becca was informing me that we had very few options left. After more than two years of living off our line of credit, she was only now on the cusp of drawing a proper salary, and we had a stack of bills a mile high. We never discussed reaching out to friends or family for help. Hosting a fund-raiser would have never crossed our minds. Instead, we called the financial advisor who had managed our IRA account before we had cashed it all out to pay medical bills, and asked him if he knew a bankruptcy attorney. He gave us a number and we made an appointment.

I sat through our meeting with the attorney and it reminded me of the doctor's visit when I received my diagnosis. I heard what

Next spread: Laying down some surf lines behind one of the all-time masters of style, Tom Burt. Mount Baker, Washington. 2018. *Colin Wiseman*

she said and hardly believed any of it. We had spent $120,000 from our line of credit. We owed roughly $380,000 on our house and it would probably sell for $525,000—if we made the decision to sell immediately. Because we were coming off the worst housing crash in US history, the value was dropping daily. After fees we would be short about $50,000. We had cashed out nearly $100,000 in retirement money, and paid the penalty fees in the process, so that we could pay off roughly $75,000 in medical bills. In the upcoming year Rebecca thought she might make $55,000 through the coffee shop. "Honestly," the woman said, "I have seen much worse. I still recommend filing for bankruptcy; it will give you a fresh start and let you begin immediately rebuilding your credit."

"We aren't looking for a fresh start," I said. "We are looking for a way to keep going." Rebecca and I thanked her for her time and left. The meeting cost us $500.

"Your parents are coming over tonight," Becca told me a few days later. "They know we are having a tough time, and they want to hear how it's going."

That night after dinner, we sat in our living room with my parents and tried to be as transparent as possible about our financial situation. I listened to Rebecca lay out the details and all I felt was embarrassed. Soon we started talking about our house and the challenges presented by living there because our location was so rural.

"The money is not even the biggest problem!" I blurted. "We can't live here because there aren't any bus routes, there's no safe way to walk anywhere, and nowhere to walk to anyway. If we stay, Madrona will begin public school for first grade and it's ten miles away. How is Rebecca going to work full time to support this family financially and also spend the rest of her life driving this family around?" I finished, my frustration at our situation coming out as anger.

"We have been looking at houses to rent on Bainbridge Island," Rebecca said calmly.

"Why there?" I heard my folks ask, and I began to retreat into myself.

As I heard the discussion continue, coldness took over my body. My parents had a lot of questions and suggestions. I became more and more angry. *Don't they know we have spent all our time looking at the angles?* I thought. But it wasn't their fault they had questions and ideas that Rebecca and I had already ruled out—it was mine. I had kept everyone around us in the dark by pretending things were fine.

I felt like a failure, like I had in high school when I hadn't met others' expectations. As I thought about this, my right hand pulled into a fist and shot upward as I punched myself in the side of my face and then, with lightning speed, did it a second time.

"Stop that!" Rebecca screamed as she grabbed my arm and tried to hold me. I heard my mom sobbing on the couch, and then I felt my dad come over and put his arm around me.

"It's all right, Son," he said. "We are going to help however we can."

The tears welled up in my eyes. "I'm tired," I said, and my folks got up to go. My dad said he would call me in the morning.

That night, I lay in bed with Rebecca. "I have never seen you like that," she said, sounding like she was going to cry.

"I just feel angry," I responded. "I am totally aware that we have a lot to be grateful for, that we still have our future, and I will work to figure things out, but I am still angry. I'm a smart guy and I know all the stuff I should do, but I just feel angry."

Rebecca put her arm across my chest and lay her head on my shoulder as I reached for my audiobook. I was listening to *The Old Man and The Sea*, my favorite book. I used to see myself as the Old Man who gets up every day to do the thing he has always done, no matter what the world throws at him. But I didn't see myself that way anymore. Instead, I felt like the giant sailfish lashed to the side of the boat, with life taking giant bites out of me on a daily basis.

In the morning my dad called. "Devon, we know you could find a place to rent, but we want to help you buy a place on Bainbridge so that Madrona and Rebecca have a stable place to live. If it's all right with you, we want to give you the down payment for a house."

I heard his words, knew how special a gift he was offering, and still I was mad at myself. "I need to give you something in exchange for the down payment, Dad," I said. "How about I give you my shares of the commercial property?"

"If you need to," he said, "but your mom and I won't do anything with them."

We put our house on the market, and a month later it sold for $505,000. A short sale was negotiated to clear the equity line, and with that sale, our credit was gone. Around the same time, I officially signed over my stake in our commercial land. And just like that, the image I held of myself as a provider was gone as well.

With the gift my parents provided we were able to move onto Bainbridge Island—an hour from where we were before. The relocation was the result of a focused search to find a home located within walking distance from every school Madrona would attend.

Hope began to whisper opportunities for a more normal existence. Town was within walking distance; so was our new pediatrician and the ferry to Seattle. All of these were accessible by sidewalks, without traffic lights, and concentrated within a mile radius.

Rebecca and I began to reestablish our own independence. She was only going to drive to and from work at our coffee shop. I would walk Madrona to school, try and stay up on the groceries, and walk anywhere I wanted to go.

After we were settled, I asked my folks to come up and walk around the area with us. I wanted to show them how accessible everything was for me. I wanted them to see what the move had done for us all and how we were rebuilding our lives.

My dad and I walked around town as I gave him a tour of the route I was becoming familiar with. "Notice how there are no traffic lights," I said. "All the intersections are four-way stops except the big roundabout up on the hill." My dad asked why that was better for me. "I can't see a flashing WALK sign across the street. But at a four-way stop I can tell if a car is there or not."

"That makes sense. I didn't think about that one," he said. When I thanked him for what he and my mom did for us, his voice softened. "You're welcome. We could see your family needed help." When I made a mumbled protest, his tone became more emphatic. "Things will get better, Devon. I know life wasn't easy for you growing up, but you have always been able to figure things out. I wish I would have let you be yourself more."

I was grateful for his faith in me. My adolescence had felt like one long battle for acceptance by my parents, but I wanted this conversation to stay light and be about how much I appreciated their support. I changed the subject away from my childhood.

"I wish I could figure out how to build houses. It's a hard thing to know exactly what you love doing and then have to look for something else. I just don't get excited about other ways of working."

"It is hard," my dad agreed. "But you will figure it out. You've always had a creative way of looking at things."

"I'm not sure you know just how creative," I said with dry sarcasm. As we headed home, I told my dad a story.

During my formative years, whenever a teacher or parent would say to me, "What do you want to be when you grow up?" I simply said, "The boss."

I have never been confined to a cubicle, and I have my first jobs to thank for that. Everything I know about business I learned from those jobs, but most importantly I learned the value of my time.

I would spend the rest of my life choosing time over money.

I wish I had known the child labor laws back then. Had I known, my playtime would have increased significantly. But as a fourth grader, with no Internet, and no legal support, I figured all kids went to work.

The paper route, as if pulled from a Norman Rockwell painting, represented a rite of passage in a young boy's life that prepared him to be a titan of industry. Paper routes were sought after by the ambitious, responsible kids. The honor was considered an early indicator that a child might become a future enterpriser or even a mogul. It seemed all parents had an idyllic view of the paper route.

I wish I had known a kid who wanted my route, because I would have given the little future enterpriser the job in an instant. My experience with it had been far from idyllic. After three years of breaking my back, I vowed the only future enterprising I would be doing would be that of my own design.

At that time in my life I didn't want a job. My mom filled out the application and then told me how excited I would be. I may have been at first, believing some cash was headed my way, but the illusion didn't last long. All the money I would earn was going directly into a savings account she had just opened for me. As a gift for opening the account I received a booklet of slotted quarters and was firmly told to save them until they increased in value, which, incidentally, has yet to happen some thirty-three years later.

My mom also tried to get me excited by saying, "You'll love this job because it lets you ride your bike all day and be outside." This was confusing because she never let me come inside anyway; quickly I realized she was selling me something I already had. *This gave me the grim feeling I might have to start paying rent soon.* I delivered those papers on my BMX bike four times a week, and did it for three years. Each delivery took me two full trips, with the bags stuffed to the max and hanging from the front bars. I had more bruises from falling off that improperly balanced bicycle than I would ever get from skateboarding or surfing. The only relief from pedaling came when it was raining or when I was overloaded with homework. During those times, one of my parents drove and I fired the papers from the passenger seat of our 240 Volvo sedan. It didn't rain much.

Once a month I was required to collect volunteer subscription fees by going door to door. The Signal had a scripted one-liner prepared in advance, which simply read, "Would you like to pay for The Signal?" My first year, I didn't give this business plan much thought. But by the second year, as a more seasoned fifth-grader, I began to question the rationale of a volunteer payment program. Why was I required to deliver newspapers to every single house and then go door to door asking if they would like to pay for the publication that I was obviously going to continue throwing on their doorstep? If someone knocked on my door and asked me to give up cash for something they were going to keep giving me anyway, I would laugh and close the door. This made me wonder if volunteers ran The Signal. I decided to check with my parents to make sure I was getting paid and to see how much was in that savings account.

I inquired about the status of my savings account, and my mom excitedly told me I had $600 safely stashed away and racking up interest at the astonishing rate of like a buck a year. Glad that I had some money, I went and flipped through the back of my Boys' Life magazine to see what I could buy. Not much, I thought.

I continued delivering The Signal for another year. Now in the sixth grade, I was actually having to prioritize my schedule. I didn't think I should put any effort into delivering a paper whose CEO favored a volunteer payment plan over what I considered the more sound "payment required for product" plan. So I decided to hang up my bags and retire from the paperboy union. After a final inquiry with my branch manager—my mom—I had $800, which she promptly told me I could use only for college. I said, "I'm not sure I'm going, and I might use the money for a surfboard." In a dry, firm voice, she responded, "You will be going to

With the bags stuffed to overflowing, I crashed often. Valencia, California. 1987.
Raney Family Collection

college," and I knew if I ever hoped to see my money, it definitely wouldn't be until I graduated high school. Walking away, I mumbled to myself, "What kind of college can I go to for eight hundred bucks anyway?"

Most of my mom's ideas were intended as ways to help me study, so I was surprised when she suggested that I sell bundles of mistletoe. She said, "During the holidays people hang bunches in their door jambs." The motor in my brain turned over and then revved up as I started thinking about the panic generally associated with Christmas—when supply and demand heat up. I figured the desire to stay festive created a demand. Becoming more interested, I asked, "Where do I get mistletoe?" Laughing, she said, "It grows on trees."

After she showed me what to look for in the treetops, I would climb up with scissors and drop large bundles of the invasive parasite to the ground. Back at home, my mom got out some red ribbon. Pulling it fast over the blade of the scissors, she showed me how to create the twist and curl. We wrapped the bundle with a bow and put it into a Ziploc bag. My mom set the original price of two dollars per bundle. I am guessing it was based off what she would pay or what she thought kids should earn. It would not remain two dollars for long.

I soon learned about the gray area. To find the real money, I would need to explore the gaps between absolute truths and malicious deception. This world is where I assumed most of the wealthy folks operate, with a convoluted moral system often referred to as "ambiguous."

As I stacked my mistletoe bundles into a cardboard box, my mom suggested I write a script so that I'd be prepared. She said, "You might want to know some key points so that you are comfortable at the door." Looking at her in bewilderment, I wondered where she thought I went every time I left to collect newspaper subscriptions. I had racked up more door-to-door experience than a seasoned Jehovah's Witness. I simply replied, "No thanks. I'll be fine."

I had solid results over the weekend. I came up with one-liners like, "It's not only mistletoe, but the hope of a kiss from someone you love." Pausing so this sank in, I rarely missed with that pitch.

I began getting the uneasy feeling that at two dollars a transaction I was not going to end the holiday season with enough money to keep me in comfort until next Thanksgiving, when I planned to start again. Not willing to accept this, I began to consider an increase in price. I was paying more attention to what was being sold on the door-to-door circuit. Sports teams were my biggest competition. I noticed that they always wore uniforms when making rounds and I knew they were selling candy bars for two dollars, the same price as me. This fact only supported an increase in price. Candy bars were gone in one sitting, but my mistletoe hung in the doorway for a month. Who knows, maybe the lonely people left it up all year. Additionally, I had to climb a tree at risk to my life. I began to understand the risk-to-reward mentality.

Acutely aware that the highest number of sales was made in support of a team or charity, I entered the gray area. I needed a team, or a charity, and if I was going to create one, why not a whole bunch of them so I could reach every demographic? I was not on any teams at the time, but I had a recent tee-ball jersey—really just a T-shirt with a number and my last name on the back—and I had the old hat as well, which completed the uniform. So I put them on and raised the price.

My first house yielded a profit that justified the hard work. When the door opened, I just said, "Selling mistletoe for the team." With a big smile, my customer said, "How much?" Prepared to drop the box and run, I replied, "Ten bucks." His reply seemed to come from heaven. "Hold on, buddy, I'll get my wallet." Walking away from the house in shock, I wondered if I was flat-out lying. I mean, maybe the team was my mom and me. Should I keep selling? It was working, so I went with it.

I sold so much mistletoe I had to start bundling it in the garage during times when I knew my mom was gone. I was buying my own ribbon, too. I was worried that if my mom saw the amount of mistletoe I was selling, she would want to know how much money I was making. The fact was, I had made more money after only a month than I did in three years of that paper route. I had close to $1,000, and no person on this planet could drag me into a bank to store that cash. I was a mattress man, and that money was safe in my room.

I kept a running record of houses I had visited and what fake charity I had used at the time. This way, after a two-week hiatus, I could return, working hard under a different cover. I also rated the charities I used so I could understand which ones were the best producers. The second-best sales came when I was working for a baseball team raising money for a tournament. I never had to name the tournament or say where we were playing. My clients never seemed to ask for the details, which made it easier to sleep at night.

Far and away the greatest generator of sales was Mexico. Knocking on the door, my pitch was simply, "I am selling mistletoe for Mexico." I believe the magic in my Hispanic falsehood was the vagueness it created. Everyone was aware of Mexico's needs, and before I could even complete my sentence, people were digging into their pockets, assuming the money was headed to build houses, clothe orphans, or provide water. Unfortunately for our brothers to the south, it just went under my mattress.

The cash cow lasted a total of four seasons. As a junior, I became too cool for climbing around in trees.

Always concerned my mom would require that I set aside a certain dollar amount for college, I never shared the extent of the operation. It was a bummer, because she would have been impressed with my commitment level, my analysis of the door-to-door market, and the work I did tracking results. I can imagine her saying, "Wow, Devon, way to keep track and do your research," followed by, "Now, quit lying and give the money back."

Once the mistletoe money under my mattress was gone, I needed a new plan. My parents provided food and a roof over my head, but they didn't hand out money. The odds were better that I would find gold in the backyard than receive a handout inside the house. So, I developed a new sales program.

Summer is a time for parties. About to be a senior in high school, I felt it was my responsibility to attend all the parties thrown that summer. Since I was broke I would bring my own keg cup, tucked under my shirt, and politely declined the suggestion to purchase one at the door. Since a keg cost big money, the host would attempt to recover his startup capital by selling keg cups for the standard ten dollars. This was the price tag on my mistletoe bundles, a realization that triggered my brain to the business opportunity presenting itself.

Keg cups were always red, and always made by the brand Solo. Once a cup was paid for, the customer could drink all night. With very little understanding of how many Solo cups a keg of beer provided, no one seemed to count how many cups were sold, or notice how an oversaturated cup market was affecting their beer supply.

A social instinct exists in the fabric of all high school kids that allows them to understand basic keg party etiquette without ever being formally taught. In the same way a cheetah cub grows tired of chasing its tail, sees a gazelle for the first time, runs it down, bites its jugular, and becomes a teenage cheetah, so it is with human teenagers who suddenly experience Friday night for the first time. They understand without words that a good party has a keg, and the only proper way to partake is with a red Solo keg cup. I could now see a summer filled with self-employment and loose hours.

As I paid attention during the following Friday-night kegger, two key things jumped out at me. First, the guy selling the red Solo cups would never last more than an hour at his post—most likely because he'd bought the keg, which meant he had been drinking from it early on. Soon he was drunk, tired of working the door, and ready to leave his post to take shots in the kitchen.

The second thing was the keg's location: Its home was always in the backyard. You had to be a new kind of stupid to change that rule. This little detail was the best part for my new venture. Creating a separate environment, the backyard was full of people who had already purchased a cup and no longer paid attention to who was selling them. This separated the herd and left the front yard strictly for newcomers, who were naturally unaware of who the rightful salesman should be anyway. As a result of this simple fact, my cover would remain intact all night.

At the next party, I came prepared with a few sleeves of Solo reds and waited for the real salesman to head for the kitchen—at which point I finished the job for him. Heading out to the front yard, I began selling like I was a hot-dog vendor at a ball game. Looking specifically for newcomers, I would say, "Keg cup. Need a keg cup?" This was not much of a pitch, but party folk often don't need any special spin on purchases that keep the party bumping. Taking a moment to identify the easy targets, or low-hanging fruit, I was pleased to realize they were everywhere. I sold my sleeves in minutes, and quickly left to count how many ten dollar bills I had stuffed in the pockets of my jeans.

Pleased with my earnings, I said to myself, This is a lot like netting salmon at the mouth of a river.

I sold cups at random parties where I was sure I only knew a few people. Unlike my mistletoe gig, the new operation required very little analysis of anything. It was simply lazy, high-return work. I was never particularly proud of the effort, but the cash could not be ignored. Eventually a friend or two wanted in, and it became like shooting fish in a barrel rather than netting them. One person directing traffic in the front yard looking official would shout, "Keg cups, side yard, keg cups, side yard!" while pointing to me. At the side yard gate I would be passing out a cup for the standard ten dollars, and saying, "Have fun, man, kegs tapped on ice." Or, to the fairer sex, I might say, "Hey, where you going after this?" However, I was always sure to treat the gals equal: ten dollars was the price and everyone paid.

After high school, I became more intentional about the location of sales and less concerned about frequency of transaction. Learning about fraternity parties, we went down to a local university. On fraternity row we provided cups to our country's future leaders: Young Republicans, the math club, the chess club; it was straight-up business. Not worried about seeing someone we knew, or whose party it was, we showed up around 11 p.m. and went home a few hours later, sold out every time.

Although I enjoyed coming up with the ideas, I was never super comfortable with my source of income. Still, it was the freedom it provided that I wanted. I was the boss. My last two gigs gave me an education most never receive and that certainly isn't found in a *minimum-wage environment. More important, I had formed a tenacity toward figuring things out.*

"Wow, Devon, I don't know if I wanted to know about that keg cup story," my dad said.

"I knew you would see it for what it was, Dad—straight-up fraud," I said, laughing. "But truthfully, selling keg cups at someone else's party, then leaving fast when the product was gone, is the closest I ever came to working in corporate America."

"What do you mean? I am pretty sure I worked in corporate America," my dad said with a challenge.

"Oh, come on, you know what I mean. If I had continued down that path I might have run a Ponzi scheme on Wall Street," I replied. "All I am saying is that my little ventures gave me the freedom I wanted—but they also showed me everything I didn't want from a career. I chose construction because I wanted to feel satisfied at the end of the day by the seeing the result of honest work I did with my hands. And then later, when I became a builder, I was proud to be transparent with what I was providing."

Early in the fall of 2011, shortly into Madrona's first-grade year at Ordway Elementary, I got a call from the school nurse. She told me that Madrona had fallen off the monkey bars and bumped her head. She was quick to say that all was well, and reading between the lines, I understood that Madrona got a little shook up and was chilling in the nurse's station for some comfort care.

When the nurse asked if I could come pick up my child from school, I was elated. *It's all working out*, I thought, opting to keep my flip-flops on and leave the Nikes for the extreme emergencies that called for a sprinting pickup. Entering the sick bay with my can-do-anything attitude, I was in high spirits. I pretended to see everything. "Hi there," I said, "I'm Devon, Madrona's dad," to a shape in the corner I figured was the nurse.

Adjusting to the environment, I recognized a bed and went to it with confidence. Getting closer, I saw the shape of a child, and arriving at the edge of the mattress, I said, "Hi, Sweetie."

I bent down and pecked her cheek and gave her a big hug. As I was doing so, I heard a familiar voice come from across the room. "Dad, I'm over here."

I didn't see that the room had two beds. Looking down at the confused recipient of a stranger's hug, I said, "Sorry, Sweetie, I don't see too good. My daughter is in here also."

Nurses at the primary grade level are strict, sometimes rigid—maybe even military-trained. So I was not surprised when the nurse in charge became standoffish after my mistake. Even after Madrona acknowledged me as her dad, things remained uncomfortable and I could feel the nurse staring at me like I was some random weirdo. It was quiet, and my chest began to tighten. For a quick second, I started to feel that oppression I remembered from the day at the zoo three years earlier. This time, though, I shook it off, apologized, and went to find the school secretary.

I wasn't as concerned anymore about how I was being received. I was there, picking up my kid without help from anyone, and I didn't care if I had to kiss the entire first grade to find her. The school secretary knew who I was, was aware of my eyesight, and was able to vouch for me. So the nurse, at the behest of her colleague, released Madrona into the custody of a man who'd hugged the wrong child.

Walking back to our house with Madrona, I was elated. The feeling of independence overpowered any embarrassment I felt in the presence of the nurse. Smiling, I said to myself, *You have to go to know.* I had been going every day in an effort to be a part of the solution to whatever new challenge presented itself on a daily basis. It finally felt like it was paying off.

Next spread: Beware of logging trucks. Cycling through Washington. 2013. *Jeff Hawe*

CHAPTER 8

It's Time for an Adventure

Settling in on Bainbridge was a huge step for all three of us. Rebecca found her independence, and Madrona began to make friends and have a more stable daily schedule. Independence returned for me as well, and I attempted to succeed at my version of the male caregiver. Again we found ourselves in a place of abundance, and at face value, things were good.

Maybe it was our new living situation that allowed me to relax and get a different perspective of the loss I'd experienced. Up to that point Rebecca and I were in survival mode. Our approach was one day at a time and one foot in front of the other.

Sometime during our second year on Bainbridge Island, I recognized a different sadness in myself. Unlike the harsh feeling of trauma, this new emotion was more of an underlying sense of loss and a gnawing awareness of things I could not control. It was a functional level of grief.

I felt disconnected from my closest friends as a result of the physical distance between us. I also felt left behind as an athlete, and it felt like years since I had been on a cool surf or snow adventure. I started paying high school kids hourly to drive me out to wherever the waves were good, and to shuttle me around for daily errands outside my comfortable walking zone. As I accepted the fact that I would always have to pay someone to take me surfing—at least until Madrona was sixteen—I felt even more lonely.

At the same time, my phone stopped ringing. I began to notice a cultural shift occurring in the way people were communicating. A new paradigm had been created by social media. I watched with despair as friends stayed connected by keeping tabs on each other through Twitter or Instagram or Facebook. The old idea of friends just hanging out had disappeared. Yet it had become normal to spend hours staring at digital representations of someone else's life.

I hoped that, over time, our culture would sense something missing and start conversing again. Soon, everyone close to me relied solely on texting. This change hit me hard. The world now required eyesight to participate in these one-way dialogues at the point in my life when I desperately needed people to speak with me. I felt like I was losing any chance I had of communicating with friends I used to talk with on the phone daily.

I needed an adventure so I could get my friends together in one place, and so I could feel the sense of connection and achievement I had known so many times before.

On a more painful level, Madrona had come home from school on two separate occasions and burst into tears. "Someone made fun of Dad's eyes," she said. More than all my other reasons, I needed an adventure to remain capable in her eyes.

———

In August of 2008, back when I had perfect eyesight, I left on a self-supported bicycle and surfing trip from Forks, Washington, to Pacific City, Oregon, 300 miles to the south. I went with Temple and our friend Forrest Burki. The trip was our first experience with long-distance bike travel, and we each chose a very different bike setup as a result. Forrest used a road bike, towing a single-wheel cargo carrier with his surfboard strapped lengthwise on top. Temple rode a hard-tail mountain bike, with his surfboard in a beach cruiser surf rack mounted to his bicycle. Without a trailer he used saddlebags on his front and rear wheels for luggage, while Forrest and I threw our clothes into the trailers we were towing. I chose my full-suspension mountain bike to tow the toddler trailer I'd been using to pull Madrona around town at the time. Additionally, I secured my surfboard alongside its outer canvas wall in a semi-vertical position like a sail.

My full-suspension bike was not suited for long road travel, and neither was my baby trailer stuffed full of more gear than I needed for a month. It was a rookie mistake, and I paid the price all day, every day, as I lagged at least a mile behind my friends at all times. My body was exhausted. My mind was also fatigued from feeling like I was holding the group back. On the third morning, I called Rebecca to pick me up.

Back home I grabbed a ten-speed road bike, tossed out half of the contents in my trailer, cut the canvas off the trailer's top, and lay my board flat over the gear. Two days later, Rebecca dropped me back off on the coast and I met up with Temple and Forrest again. The three of us finished in Pacific City.

I had never bailed on an adventure before. It was the first time I needed to call for a pickup and go home to change my gear. I was embarrassed; I felt I had let my friends down.

While driving back to Washington, I made a promise to myself that someday I would return and pedal the entire US West Coast with a surfboard. A month later I hit my head, began to lose my vision, and stopped dreaming about any future adventures.

I purchased a tandem road bike in 2010, and I had two solid years of pedaling it with a friend of mine, Dr. Tom Herron, up front in the captain's seat. After rebuilding my confidence on the back of that bike, I started to believe the trip might still be possible. That promise to myself to ride the whole West Coast was the seed that eventually became the Bikes, Boards, Blind surf trip.

My cycling partnership with Tom continued on Bainbridge, with him showing up twice a week to go cycling with me despite the sixty-mile drive from Gig Harbor. I was deeply affected by his commitment. The dream grew some more and I wondered if Tom would want to pedal up front all the way to Tijuana.

Tom Herron was a huge source of encouragement to me during those early years of my eye diagnosis. Sometimes I would burst out laughing when I remembered the way I first met him.

I was required by law to have a portable toilet on my lot during construction. I ignored the rule because I was young, building my first house, and counting every penny. As it turns out, being cheap not only saves money but also provides interesting ways to meet new people.

There was no way for me to have known that the man preparing to poop in my yard would, a decade later, become a mentor to me and a spectacular source of hope to both Rebecca and me during the hardest time of our life.

Rebecca and I had purchased the waterfront land and were building our first house, which Rebecca had designed and drawn to scale. The project produced the best creative thinking I have ever done. It turns out many of the scams I ran as a youth were, in at least a few ways, time well spent. They taught me to see risk as a good thing and to creatively find solutions no matter what. But over the years, I had developed a rigid commitment to the truth.

For our construction loan, I wanted to borrow the least amount possible. But the bank needed to see that the money I was requesting was enough to build a house. I found my creative solution by using vague statements that were truthful but still had an element of hustle. For the concrete cost, I wrote, "Not a problem, a friend owes me a favor." For the heating system, "My father-in-law Larry is a mechanical engineer. He's got it covered." The bank approved the loan.

Rebecca was finishing up her degree at UW and I was working full-time as project manager for Hendrickson Construction, so all the work was done on weekends and in the evenings.

I was ill-prepared for the confusing social exchange a yard pooping can create. It was a Saturday when I first laid eyes on Tom Herron. Throughout that previous week I had worked in the evenings to install roof trusses on our home, and it was my task that Saturday to put the plywood sheeting on those trusses. Sometime around midmorning, I came down off the roof for a break and sat inside under a window cutout to eat my sandwich and look around the interior of my castle. I heard a rustle in the bushes outside, but I was tired and didn't want to stand up to check it out. The bushwhacking continued and sounded like a dog circling before a big dump. Laboring to get up, I stood and poked my head outside. There crouched a man with his running shorts down to his knees. This dude doesn't look homeless or destitute, *I thought to myself.*

"Hey man, what are you doing!" I shouted. He looked up at me, a bit frustrated at the interruption and still crouching.

"Where is the porta-potty?" he asked.

His inquiry reminded me of the rule I was breaking by not having a portable restroom and I didn't want to be reminded of this. I shouted, "I don't have one!"

The runner pulled up his shorts, and I watched with slight bemusement as he sprung from the bushes onto the pavement with the agility of a feral jungle cat. Seconds later he was sprinting up the road, with primordial urgency. Dang, I thought to myself, that dude is fit. Once we moved into the house, I learned from neighbors that he lived around the corner. I would see him running on a regular basis and but never learned his name.

Four years later, Becca and I were taking our infant daughter Madrona for her first doctor visit. The pediatrician introduced himself. Wondering if there was a hidden camera and I was being pranked, I thought to myself, What? This dude is the runner from my yard.

He was wearing a white coat instead of jogging shorts and possessed a demeanor far more professional than when we'd last spoken, but I recognized him right away.

"Congratulations on becoming parents. I'm Tom Herron, it's nice to meet you," he said to us. This is awesome, I thought, but I remained silent during the examination, wondering if he recognized me. I didn't bring it up with Tom that day because I didn't want Becca to have an awkward memory attached to her baby girl's first checkup.

"We have the best doctor ever," I told Rebecca as we left. I was simply thrilled our pediatrician was comfortable pooping in the woods.

That same year I had taken up running. With a baby at home, I wanted to be around as much as possible, and running provided a good workout in a relatively short time. So I accepted the fact that I would have to wear the lame shorts, and show the world how hairy my legs truly are.

I ran daily. On one of my first longer runs, a ten-mile loop, I began to experience what I assumed was going on with Tom the day he was searching for a porta-potty. At mile six, I could feel my bowels turning to liquid. So I ran off the trail and into the deeper brush, and returned minus one sock.

Returning home with only one sock, I explained to my wife what had happened. "My first sock sacrifice as a jogger," I said proudly, although I had certainly used the technique on other adventures. Rebecca, the more practical money spender in the household, wryly responded, "Then you don't need to buy a pair of thirty-dollar running socks if you're going to wipe your ass with one of them." Great point!

Three years passed before I accompanied Becca on one of Madrona's checkups. This time things were very different for us as a family. I was there because I was no longer driving or working.

During the appointment, the clinic manager came to do a simple eye exam on Madrona. Her name is Verna, and we learned that she is Dr. Herron's wife. Moving us into the hallway, she set Madrona in front of a children's eye chart. Hoping no one noticed, I positioned myself alongside my daughter and began testing myself. I didn't get one thing right.

Showing us back to the room, Verna said, "So, how are you guys doing?" I felt like she really wanted to know and was not just making small talk. I could no longer answer "fine," so I laid it all out for her. Becca and I both shared all we could handle.

Verna asked how she could help. Having made the connection previously that Verna is an avid runner, I told her I was still running. Then I explained how I needed a guide simply to run next to me. Without hesitation, Verna offered to be one of those people.

So, I began running most mornings alongside the wife of the man who almost pooped in my yard. Of course, I never spoke of that day with Verna.

While we ran, she would often speak of cycling and the trips she and Tom took. Traveling with their road bikes they spent quality time, sharing their passion together. It made me think of Becca and all the snowboarding we had experienced as a couple.

Although Rebecca and I never stopped going to the beach or the mountains, I was having a hard time staying active when I needed quick exercise at home. Fearful that my new reality was going to significantly limit the ways I could exercise, I purchased a tandem road bike and contacted an organization of blind triathletes. The conversation was super informative, and the group remained a source of support anytime I needed information on fitness techniques for the blind.

Soon after buying the tandem, I shared the news with Verna while on a morning run and told her I was looking for someone to captain the bike. Verna was stoked and promised to pass on the idea to her husband. Tom offered to cycle with me, and a few days later I had my first real conversation with him. From there, I spent many hours sitting behind the runner I had met in my bushes seven years earlier.

Tom called me almost every weekday to see if I was available for a ride on the tandem. He is nearly twenty years older than me and cycling is his passion. I believe on many of those days he would have preferred a ride in solitude on his own bike. That he would check with me before going solo was such a powerful gesture that I could never say no. As a result, I learned to say yes again, during a time when I wanted to say no to everything.

He understood a few things about me. As a father, he intuitively recognized the fear I was carrying on a daily basis. I was scared that my daughter Madrona would be ridiculed because of my disability, and I did not see a clear picture in my head of how I was going to be the fun dad I had always envisioned.

Many times while on the back of the tandem, I shared with Tom how difficult it was to lose my independence once I stopped driving and also the constant pain I felt relying on other people to pick Madrona up from school. He agreed that the daily reminders of my loss would be hardest for him as well.

He then proceeded to describe the tag-along bicycle designed for kids. This device is meant to be towed behind a regular bicycle and is made up of a back wheel, seat, pedals that spin freely, fixed handlebars, and a long neck reaching from the wheel that can be clamped to the seat post of almost any bike. I went out and bought one right away.

Every other week or so, Tom would leave his pediatric clinic at 3 p.m. so that we could pedal the tandem bike up to Madrona's school by 3:45 and pick her up from kindergarten. With the tag-along attached to the back, my tandem road bike became almost twenty feet long. The first time I showed up at school and handed Madrona her bike helmet, she was speechless as she stared at the three-person contraption that was longer than most full-sized trucks. But I was elated, the happiest dad in the pickup line, and the victory simply strengthened my belief that a unique solution existed for everything.

Tom would occasionally sign the two of us up for the organized distance rides he enjoyed so much. These hundred-mile rides are known to cyclists as centuries. Just like runners strive to complete a marathon, avid cyclists strive to complete a century. The Washington rides were exceptional, and I fondly remember pedaling behind Tom in the Tour de Kitsap and the High Pass Challenge. I also enjoyed the shorter race rides with steep uphill climbs like the Mt. Baker Hill Climb.

I experienced parts of Washington in a new way during those hundred-mile bike events. I had previously known those areas only from the inside of a car, and only during winter on my way to snowboard. On those summer days I smelled the cedar, fir, and pine trees and got a greater sense of how vast our Washington forests are. We did not limit ourselves to Washington. We drove the tandem down to pedal in the Santa

A trailer cycle behind a tandem—it doesn't get much longer than this. Tom Herron points the way for me and Madrona in Nelson, British Columbia. 2010. *Rebecca Raney*

Barbara Century. Months later, we put the bike on the back of Tom's Suburban and drove north to ride through Nelson, British Columbia.

My favorite ride was when we pedaled up 10,000 feet on the thirty-mile road to the top the Haleakala Volcano on the island of Maui. I remember being at 9,000 feet with the summit in view and feeling the snap of a chain link. Stunned, I couldn't believe we had flown all the way to Hawai'i and rented Maui's only tandem road bike only to have a broken chain stop us in our tracks. Damn, if I would have shipped my tandem bike with us this wouldn't have happened, *I thought* to myself. *Sitting next to the bike, both of us looked up as we heard a shaky voice say, "Excuse me, do you guys have anything to eat?" Broken down and without any food, a cyclist needed help. "Sure!" we replied and gave him one of our peanut butter sandwiches. Then we asked him, "Do you have an extra chain link?" With enthusiasm he said, "Sure!" Tom fixed the chain on the rental, and we summited an hour later.*

Although I didn't know it then, Tom was helping me rekindle the dream I harbored of cycling the entire West Coast. Our time together on that bike laid the framework for what would become one of the coolest adventures of my life. And Tom Herron would be an integral part of that adventure, as he would pedal over 600 miles for his portion as captain of the tandem.

Over the next few years, I learned a new technique for almost everything. But it was cycling with Tom on my tandem bike that taught me the type of help I really needed. I needed help staying active.

Grateful for a riding partner, and not wanting to make things awkward, it took me a while to ask Tom if he remembered that day in my yard. At first he said, "Vaguely," but soon he came clean and laughed, saying, "I remember, Devon."

Tom Herron has won Best Doctor awards too many times to count. He and Verna have raised four boys who still like hanging with them. Someday, given Tom's influence and many friendships, there will likely be a party held in his honor—possibly a retirement party, or a Physician of the Year gala—I can see it all in my mind's eye, and it looks something like this:

I'm wearing a tuxedo and look three inches taller. Rebecca is in a floor-length black gown and wearing a diamond necklace. There will be lots of people and, of course, champagne. Maybe a few senators. At some point the host, who will probably be famous, will announce, "Now is the time to share stories you have about our guest of honor, Tom Herron." I will wait patiently, allowing everyone else to go before me. At last I'll casually walk to the microphone. Looking dapper, speaking slowly with the articulation of a great leader, I will begin with, "Let me tell you all about the time Tom Herron almost pooped in my yard."

Rebecca and I began regularly discussing the adventure and what seventy-five days without me at home would look like. Soon we were talking about it so frequently that I just assumed she wanted me to go. As we continued to bounce around ideas, it became obvious how big the undertaking was and how many people would need to be involved to get it off the ground. I was coming up with new trip concerns daily: How can we stack two surfboards? What size boards will fit best? Is the tandem going to need mechanical work? How many tubes do we need to bring? Do we need to bring extra tires? How do we replace disk brakes on the road? Should we create a list of towns along the way with bike shops? Does the captain need clip-in shoes? What if we get perfect surf somewhere—do we stay and add miles the next day or just add a day of float in each leg? These questions stacked up daily, and I asked my dad to help Rebecca with the planning.

Becca organized much of the logistics with the help of my dad: daily mileage, finding good surf spots and campsites, transportation in and out for the captains, the number of days per leg.

I spent my time going on tandem bike rides and surfing as much as possible. It all felt good, and working with Becca on a project again felt like the glory days when she designed a house and I built it.

The positive energy surrounding the dream began to grow exponentially. My dad was driving me every other day to surf where the waves were good. I had also contacted a few bicycle clubs on Bainbridge, and random people were volunteering to cycle with me for training rides. After a few months we had an itinerary that looked like this:

Trip Leg 1 – Captain: Temple Cummins
Bainbridge Island to Westport, Washington
Friday, September 6 – Friday, September 13

Trip Leg 2 – Captain: Scott Gravatt
Westport, Washington, to Pacific City, Oregon
Sunday, September 15 – Friday, September 20

Trip Leg 3 – Captain: Tom Herron
Pacific City, Oregon, to Bodega Bay, California
Sunday, September 22 – Friday, October 4

Trip Leg 4 – Captain: Mike Cummins
Bodega Bay to Santa Cruz, California
Sunday, October 6 – Friday, October 11

Next spread: Northwest surfing: cold, clean, and fun. Moclips, Washington. 2017. *Rebecca Raney*

Trip Leg 5 – Captain: Tom Burt
Santa Cruz to San Luis Obispo, California
Sunday, October 13 – Friday, October 18

Trip Leg 6 – Captain: Ron Hendrickson
San Luis Obispo to Carpinteria, California
Sunday, October 20 – Friday, October 25

Trip Leg 7 – Captain: Blake Raney
Carpinteria, California, to Tijuana, Mexico
Sunday, November 3 – Wednesday, November 13

Everything looked organized. I had my dream team of athletes assigned to each leg, and now all I needed to do was call the guys and see if they were in. I made the calls and everyone said, "Yes."

The scope of my adventure had grown to a point that I was no longer in control of it. I accepted this with reluctance at first, but I soon became more open to input. Because of my aversion to social media, I initially resisted the idea of any sort of online presence for the adventure. But I had asked for help from my dad and Rebecca, and so I respectfully listened as they both lobbied heavily for a blog.

Rebecca made her case often and in the pleasant, subtle way a loving partner knows is effective. Becca would broach the subject saying, "Madrona is going to be without you for over two months. Are you going to have the energy and patience to tell her over the phone all that's happened that day? If you want her to know how awesome the adventure truly is, then you need to write in a journal daily or just use a blog."

My dad had a similar opinion and shared it by saying often, "Family members want to know how it's going. If you don't have a way to update them, then they'll just call me for two months. Devon, don't make me field those calls for you." Then we both laughed at the thought of my dad, with his relaxed, even-keeled

Opposite: The trailer broke down more often than the bike. Tom Burt changing a flat somewhere south of Santa Cruz, California. 2013. *Jeff Hawe*

persona, answering calls every day from relatives wondering how many miles I had gone and if I was stopping by their town even though it was 400 miles inland. Slowly their point settled in.

The final straw that broke my opposition to the blog was the encouragement we received from Madrona's upcoming third-grade teacher, Boo Schneider. "If you have any sort of trip blog, please let me know," Boo said. "I think the third-graders could benefit from hearing your story, and I would be willing to start each day by pulling up your blog and tracking your progress."

Since she seemed to think it would stoke the kids, I saw the blog in a different light. We planned to use a beacon every night to post our GPS coordinates, which would show up as a red dot on a map. Boo could then use these tools to have Madrona's class follow our journey.

With Madrona's class following our blog, I hoped the attention would keep her engaged in my adventure on a daily basis and distract her from my absence. Within the week, bikesboardsblind.com was formed.

With the purchase of our blog name came the monthly fee to keep it active and a template to show Becca how to create it. The template suggested a video section, a photo section, a trip description, and a home page. Soon Becca was putting up our itinerary, a video of me speaking about my vision impairment, and a trip mission statement.

One of the most common questions I received after the blog went up was, "What are you raising money for? What is the cause?" The question popped up frequently throughout the trip and still does today when someone hears about the adventure for the first time.

I have never had any cause associated with my Bikes Boards Blind adventure. Often, people assumed we were fund-raising because of my vision impairment and the team effort.

The collaboration with great friends, the chance to build something with Rebecca, the test of physical fortitude, the sense of achievement, the need to generate a sense of pride in my daughter, and the search for good waves were the only reasons I left for Tijuana on a tandem bike. From the beginning, the idea held a powerful sense of hope for me and I shared that often, but it never had anything to do with raising money.

However, some generous financial gifts were made by a few family members and close friends. As Rebecca arranged for plane tickets for captains and started to book lodging for the trip, the huge financial undertaking became apparent. These people simply wanted to see the adventure come together successfully and not become a burden in the process.

Although the blog may have added more grandeur than I intended, it also offered the chance to clarify our mission. I spent a lot of effort making it clear that "The Trip" in itself was "The Reason."

Just to see how well we could juggle, we threw in another component at the last minute. At Madrona's elementary school carnival, I received the most intriguing suggestion yet from the school principal. He said, "You should speak at high schools along the way. I think it would be really powerful for the kids to understand you are actually on your adventure when you pull off the highway and walk into the gym dirty and sweaty with your tandem bike, boards, and gear: it might give them a slight sense of participation. That would have been the coolest assembly I ever went to as a high schooler."

Something about his words resonated with me. I had spent a lifetime feeling like I didn't fit in at school. Maybe speaking at high schools could be an opportunity to pay respect to the institution I had chosen to turn my back on as a teenager. I asked myself, *Is it possible to share the adventure by simply showing up and discussing the trip without preaching any message?* I wasn't sure if speaking was for me; it felt like a lot of pressure to give a motivational speech. Still, I recognized it was a rare opportunity for me to give a respectful nod to education and also show Madrona a bigger picture by sharing the experience with high schoolers.

A few days after the carnival, I contacted Ocosta Junior/Senior High School in Westport and asked if they felt there was any value in hearing from a couple of surfers on a tandem bike headed for Mexico. On the other end of the phone I heard, "Yes, definitely." I hung up and thought, *That was cool.* Located along the coast of Washington and at the end of Leg 1, we added Ocosta to the itinerary.

Next spread: Tom Herron and me cycling down the Oregon coast. 2013. *Jeff Hawe*

CHAPTER 9

Bikes, Boards, Blind

On Wednesday, September 4, 2013, my phone rang. When I answered, I heard Temple's voice. "It looks like there's going to be waves on Friday," he said. "Can you leave a day early?"

"I'm pretty much ready now," I responded.

"OK, let's leave tomorrow. I can be at your house in the afternoon."

As I got off the phone I smiled. *You are scrambling and rearranging already,* I said to myself. *It's going to be a great trip.*

The following day I waited for Madrona to bike home from school and then kissed her good-bye. I gave the same love to Rebecca and then climbed on the back of our freshly tuned-up tandem road bicycle. "I'm ready," I said to Temple, and we lit out for the Mexico border. More accurately, we left for Sequim, Washington, where we would spend the first night.

It didn't take long before I heard the familiar sound of Temple's laugh. "What?" I asked.

"This thing reminds me of a canoe. Super tippy and with power in the back."

In no time we hit the Agate Pass Bridge, marking our departure from Bainbridge Island. A photographer from the *Kitsap Sun* waited on the opposite side to take our photo. As we blew past him, he waved his arms and shouted something.

"I think that guy wanted to ask us some questions," I said, laughing.

"We haven't been going long enough to stop yet," Temple replied, and I felt his legs push harder as the bike accelerated.

I smiled. *The trip is on,* I thought.

The afternoon began to fade. We pedaled into dusk and I broke our silence. "Do you remember when we found that dead body?" I said.

"How could I forget?" Temple responded sarcastically.

I agreed. "Over the past few years I have thought about that day a bunch," I continued.

Temple Cummins entered the elite ranks of professional snowboarding in his late teens. As a result, he not only accomplished the rare feat of becoming a paid athlete, but he also became a homeowner before the age of twenty.

Temple's home was on the beach along a stretch of water known as Colvos Passage, in Washington's Puget Sound. Originally, it was a small cabin, backed up against a steep bank and facing east with a majestic view of Mount Rainier. Later, he added a second story and the small cabin became a full-blown house. From his deck you could see most all of Commencement Bay, parts of Vashon Island, and the Tacoma city lights at night. I spent a lot of time there, fascinated by the surroundings and in awe of the Puget Sound. It was an environment far from boring. We were always paddling something: a kayak, canoe, or paddleboard was always within reach. The Sound was quickly proving to be a playground for me, and it was obvious I could go a lifetime exploring the region and still not see it all. Any chance I got, I would sleep on his deck or in the sand on the beach.

A few years later, when Becca and I built our own house along a different stretch of water, Hale Passage, I did my best to repeat the magic on our beach; kayaks, a rowboat, and paddleboards were always available. Soon I was the proud owner of a seventeen-foot Boston Whaler, and I kept it on a buoy out in front of our home. I would go everywhere on that boat, always stopping by Temple's. Boat travel had now become a way of life and it provided a new level of freedom. Running my boat up on the beach wherever I wanted to explore, or just going from one city to another without a car, is a special thing. When the sound of a ninety-horsepower two-stroke motor got old, I would enjoy the quiet and solace my kayak provided.

Eventually Madrona was born and we sold our waterfront house so that we could move on to different projects. As a result, I began renting

a boat slip at an old fisherman's net shed in downtown Gig Harbor. There I parked our Boston Whaler as well as my kayak. By the time Madrona turned two, I had already been taking her on kayak excursions with me. On Sundays, I'd bundle her up in her toddler life jacket, put her on my lap, paddle out the mouth of Gig Harbor, and head north. In forty-five minutes we'd be at Temple's house. We'd have a quick breakfast followed by a return paddle to his family's snowboard shop back in town, where he worked a shift every Sunday. I went up to his house by way of kayak on Sunday mornings for years, a constant in my world when most everything else changed often.

I really don't remember why, but I'd left Madrona home the day I found the dead body. It was a Sunday like every other, and I paddled up to Temple's house around 10 a.m. He was serving his son Cannon pancakes. I ate a few myself, and soon breakfast was over.

Preparing to leave, Temple took his kayak down from its rack, we said good-bye to his family, and I slid back into my kayak. Pushing off, we fought the current while staying a hundred or so yards offshore.

Maybe I was daydreaming, or maybe we were talking, but what I remember for sure was the delayed reaction I had as I stared at what looked to be a person floating lifelessly. I blinked a few times as I paddled toward the bobbing corpse. He was facedown and obviously dead.

The man was still fully clothed and wearing his shoes, an old pair of Skechers. His pants were black Levi's and he was wearing a rock concert T-shirt; I don't remember the band. The dead body was swollen, but I couldn't tell if it was just his shape or from the hours spent in salt water.

Staring at him, we had begun to drift in the current, so I took a rope, lashed him to the side of my boat, and towed him to shore. At the beach, Temple and I pulled our kayaks out and then stood in silence. The body was only halfway on the sand, legs and hips still floating. Wind chop lapped the beach, flexing the man in a way that was unnatural and unsettling, so I pulled him all the way up. He had a bunch of seaweed hanging from the side of his mouth and lots of sand around his nostrils, like he had fallen face first into the sand and took a deep breath.

Opposite: Standup paddling with Madrona as my eyes. Bainbridge Island, Washington. 2012. *Rebecca Raney*

I got my cell phone from my kayak and made the call to 911. The call turned out to be more challenging than I expected. We were on the beach away from any roads, and the 911 operator didn't have a clue how to find us. She kept asking me the nearest cross street, and I kept telling her to get a chart. I decided to forget about boating directions or nautical terms, and so I switched to driving instructions.

"Tell the Gig Harbor boat cop to drive out the mouth of Gig Harbor and turn left," I said, "then go one mile and look left toward shore; that is where we are." It took a long time and an additional phone call with dispatch to get them to our location.

While we waited, I thought about how when I am in the wilderness, whether it be on the water or in the mountains, I couldn't rely on anyone to take care of me. I realized my perception that help was always on the way had been largely inflated.

As the tide went out, the dead body began to completely rest on the sand. All that was left to do was wait, and I grew restless and uneasy. I started to wonder what would I say if some folks stopped by on a beach walk. "Just towed this guy to shore. Don't think there's much we can do for him. Enjoy the rest of your walk." I laughed out loud and shared my thought with Temple. Soon we began openly speculating about how the deceased came to be floating in our waters. Did he fall out of his boat or, even more likely, off a party boat or booze cruise?

During this exchange of random scenarios, we noticed an old rope swing hanging from a large branch. We jumped up and grabbed it at the same time. The slope of the beach gave us a natural push, and holding on in tandem, we flew barely a foot above the dead body. I thought the rope might snap and drop us on the dead guy's chest, but it held. We were like kids, giggling at first, then laughing uncontrollably. Is it wrong to goof off this much while a dead body is lying right below me? *I wondered.* Letting go of the rope, I stood on the beach and continued laughing uncontrollably. Like always, laughter became my default emotion.

I had always assumed that if I ever came in contact with a dead body I would behave in a somber way. As it turned out, I didn't act the way I thought I would at all. I didn't really feel much of anything, and realizing this made me uncomfortable. Looking at the man who lay lifeless in the sand, I kept hoping that a profound sense of something would hit me.

When the boat police arrived, I stared in bewilderment as they stepped ashore wearing wetsuits. Is that why it took them so long— they had to put on their wetsuits? *I asked myself.*

I knew what a body bag was but had never actually seen one. Roll-
ing the man in and zipping it up, the cops did their work. The sobering
weight of forever finally took hold of me.

What happened next made it all real and forced me to address what
I hadn't so far. The police boat turned around, with its bow out to sea
and its stern to shore. I watched—transfixed—as they dragged the hu-
man garment bag down the beach into waist-deep water and then up
onto the swim platform. The body bent weirdly, half on the step and
half in the water. The divers got completely into the boat and pulled the
corpse the rest of the way using the stairs. Even in the body bag I could
see the shape of the guy's head. It smacked every step on the way up,
like a Slinky in reverse.

The next day I learned the reason we found the man floating in
the water. Unfortunately, he had ended his own life by jumping off the
Tacoma Narrows Bridge, six miles south of where we found him.

"A permanent solution to a temporary problem," Temple said
gravely. I remember thinking how accurate the statement was. My eye
diagnosis would come a few years later, and not long after that I would
go through a stretch of time where I experienced the complete absence
of hope. When I could, I would try to remind myself that no matter how
hard things felt, my problems were only temporary.

"What is it about that day that gets you?" Temple asked.

"That whole thing makes me think of different things at different times," I said. "Sometimes I remember how fun your house
on the water was and how my appreciation for the Puget Sound
grew from those early days. Most of what I know about Washington I learned from you. Other times, when I think of that day, I
think about the suicide victim," I continued. "The mental stuff is
horrible, and probably super hard to recognize. I've been through
some shit, and when I think about that guy, I just feel fortunate
that my mind is holding strong."

"Yeah, for sure." Temple added, "Mental illness is crazy hard
to comprehend. Take my body, but leave me my mind."

"Wow, you have all the sage wisdom going on right now," I
said laughingly.

"Should we stop at the Alderwood Bistro?"

"Do you really have to ask?" I said. We leaned the long bicycle
against the back wall of the restaurant and went in for a gourmet

meal. Saying hello to our friend who worked there, we ordered more than we could eat.

Both of us were cold from our time sitting down, but we climbed back into position on the bike. We had five more miles to go and it was well past dark. "No lights?" Temple asked.

I smiled. "I guess not. I was trying to keep weight down. Doesn't the bike feel light to you?" I said with a chuckle.

"Oh yeah, super light."

The bike ran silent and smooth along the bluff that defines the Sequim region. The bluffs act as a stretch of shoreline in the Strait of Juan de Fuca. The body of water runs east/west over the top of Washington and separates the state from Vancouver Island, British Columbia. Soon we were pedaling a section near the edge of the bluff and parallel with the Strait. I could smell the salt water.

"Stopping!" Temple shouted. It's the job of the captain to call this out whenever he stops the bike abruptly. Otherwise, the stoker—the rider in back—might keep pedaling forcefully. Since the pedals work in unison, it could be dangerous if the two riders fall out of sync. We both put our right foot down. "There's a lightning storm brewing out over the water," he said. "It's mostly over the south end of Vancouver Island, but I think it's blowing this way." I looked north in that direction out of habit. I could tell through the sides of my eyes that the night sky was clear of clouds and dark.

"There was a good one," Temple said. "Did you see any of that?"

"Not yet," I said.

"They are getting brighter," he said. I was totally happy just standing there, peacefully, and listening to the waves hit the bluff below. The two of us stared out over the water and waited.

"Oh yeah," I said a few minutes later. "I saw that flash." Another one, now brighter, flashed out over the water. "I can't see the bolt, but the flash lights up everything around me, and my peripheral catches the stark contrast. It's rad," I said.

We watched some more and then pushed off to finish the ride. "That was probably the only visual experience we've been able to share today," Temple said.

I smiled. "Yeah, but it was awesome, and it's one more than we shared yesterday."

The swell came in like we'd hoped, and in the morning we went surfing. The following day we surfed again, a little farther west, and on the third day we turned south and pedaled out to the beach known as La Push on the western coastline. It was dark when we arrived and started pulling our sleeping gear from the bike trailer.

The trailer was a two-wheeled rectangular cargo unit that attached to the back of the bike. It was stuffed with two sleeping bags, two bivy sacks, two pads, two wetsuits, two pairs of booties, a pot, a pan, a Jetboil stove, a random selection of food, a camera, some flip-flops, some surf wax, honey, coffee, a container of cream, and as much water as we could store. A canvas enclosure was stretched over it and our two six-foot surfboards rested horizontally on top, strapped down with two bungee cords and one nylon tie-down. The miniature U-Haul weighed eighty pounds and the entire rig ran sixteen feet. On the front wheel of the tandem we had two small panniers stuffed with clothing.

It took only minutes before we were soaked from the thick coastal drizzle. I grabbed a wool top from my pannier and threw our bivy sacks out on the sand. We pushed our sleeping bags inside the claustrophobic bivies. After a sleepless hour went by, I got out of my bag and went for a walk. Temple was sitting outside his bag as well. "It's crazy," he said. "My bivy keeps the drizzle out but keeps my sweat in. I'm so sticky I can't sleep in that thing."

"Mine is doing the same thing," I said. "And mine smells like cat piss, too. It's weird—I can't remember where I had it stored, but something has been living in that thing," I grumbled. Neither of us slept much.

In the morning, we rolled up our sleeping bags and repacked them in the bike trailer. Then we took our bivy sacks over to the dumpster and threw them away. "Let's go for a surf," Temple said.

Soon we were back on the bike and cycling out to the 101 Highway. "There's a logging road up ahead," Temple said. "It's a fifteen- or seventeen-mile bypass."

"I'm good with it," I replied. "It will at least keep us off the main road for a bit."

We turned right, and the road, the Goodman Mainline, was dirt, washboard style, one lane with just enough width for a semi to travel in one direction, and flat at the beginning. We hadn't gone long when Temple said, "I'm stopping," and I felt him slow the bike. "Hold the bike," he said, and then he ran into the bushes. I steadied the bike and waited. Ten minutes later Temple walked back to the bike. When he got alongside me I could tell that he was stretching his T-shirt out in front of him and using it like a salad bowl. I tilted my head down to see what he was carrying. "Chanterelles," he said.

"No way," I replied, and I reached my hand in to feel the mushrooms. "Those are nice ones," I said. "They aren't soggy at all." Temple gently packed the coveted fungi into a side pouch of the trailer.

"Dinner," he said.

Soon the dirt road became hilly and our work began as we pedaled hard to keep our speeds up on the gravel surface. Logging trucks were passing us on a regular basis, either coming directly at us or mowing us down from behind. We could hear their compression brakes long before they reached us, and we always pulled the bike off to the side. A few didn't slow at all. "I am not sure they want a couple of surfers taking a tandem cruise on their road," I said. "It's too late now, though."

In the early afternoon, the road leveled out as we reached the ridgeline. The sky opened up, a result of all the logging that had been going on, and when the semis were absent the only sounds I heard were birds and the pinging sound our bike tires made when they shot a small piece of gravel off to the side. It wasn't long before my idyllic nature daydream was shattered by the sound of a compression brake. Temple steered the bike off to the left and we looked back to watch the truck as it approached. "This guy is slowing down a lot," Temple said. The logging truck came to a stop right beside us. "He's rolling down his window," Temple said. We both craned our necks upward.

A purebred logger stuck his head out and said, "You boys missing anything?" Temple and I looked at each other; instantly my mind began to race as I tried to think of anything we might be missing. Maybe we were missing a permit to pass on this road. Or maybe he just thought we were missing our minds.

"This dude is going to kick some surfer ass," I whispered.

"I don't think we are missing anything," Temple responded.

"I can't think of anything either," I added.

The man started laughing. "Are you sure?" he asked.

He has an honest laugh, like a craftsman, I thought to myself, and for a brief instant I felt like I was on the job site building houses again. Temple and I just stared up at the guy dumbly.

"Alright," he said, still laughing, "I'll just give 'em to ya." Then he dangled two wetsuits out the window of his cab. Temple looked back at our bike trailer.

That morning, after our surf, we'd chosen to slide our wetsuits under the straps that held our surfboards tightly to the trailer. Normally we packed the wetsuits safely inside the canvas walls, but our hope was that if they were on top they would dry out in the sun and wind. Instead, they fell off as we bounced down a dirt road.

"You are super awesome," I said.

"You boys would be cold out there without these, wouldn't ya?" he said.

"Thank you so much," Temple said. "How far back were they?"

"I found them in the middle of the road at mile six," the man replied. "Alright, you boys take it easy and be safe," he said as he put his truck in gear and lumbered forward.

That night we slept in the grass next to the compostable toilets at a day-use-only state park on Ruby Beach. We lay our sleeping bags up tight to the building under the protection of the roof overhang and boiled water for noodles. We sautéed our chanterelle mushrooms in butter, then mixed it all together with a jar of red sauce. Our bellies full, we both slept soundly that night.

Three days later we arrived in Westport, Washington. Rebecca had rented us a condo on VRBO near the harbor and Temple found it with ease. "Let's put the bike in the parking garage and then walk out to the jetty and check the surf," I said. There were waves and we got in the water.

Our families drove down that evening and soon I was catching up with Rebecca and Madrona. Temple did the same with his wife, Barrett, son, Cannon, and daughter, Ayla. A dinner plan began to form and I smiled as I realized how glad we all were to see each other.

In the morning, Temple and I put the bike rig back together and pedaled to the Westport high school—the first of eight schools I would visit on our trip. At the assembly, I shared an

Camping with Temple Cummins in the Washington drizzle. Our board bags turned out to be the best shelter. Ocean Shores, Washington. 2013. *Temple Cummins Collection*

unscripted presentation about what our adventure meant to me. I gave a brief explanation of my eye condition and heard murmurs as the kids made the connection between my vision impairment and the bicycle with two seats propped on the stage. I finished by saying, "I have had to work hard to find new ways to do the things I love, but if you look hard enough there is usually a solution." Then I opened it up for questions.

"How are you getting all that stuff back from Mexico?" one kid asked.

"That is a great question. My wife and daughter are going to meet us at the end of the trip in Tijuana with our truck, and we'll load it all in and drive back together."

"How do you dial the phone?" a kid asked.

"I have to use a raised keypad," I explained. "Not a touch screen. On the number five of every raised keypad is a braille dot.

I feel for this dot on the number five, and then I dial any number I want around it by memory."

A girl stood up from her seat and said, "You look really good." Instantly a few snickers could be heard. "I mean you dress nice," she clarified. "How do you do that? Do you dress yourself?"

"Yes, I still dress myself," I said, trying to hold back a laugh. "I generally wear jeans, which has been the case for a long time now, so I know the zipper goes in front. I mostly wear T-shirts and zip-up jackets, but occasionally I have to wear a button-up shirt and I know from when I had perfect vision that those buttons go in front as well."

Now there was lots of laughter in the bleachers, and so I announced it was time for us to go. "I want to thank all of you for having us here today," I said. "It's been awesome." The school principal came up and thanked us, and then we pushed the bike out of the school gym.

"That was fun," I said as we pedaled back to the rental condo.

"Yeah, and funny," Temple added genuinely.

In the afternoon, Temple sorted out his gear and loaded it into their truck. "Alright," he said. "We're out of here."

I gave him a hug. "Thank you for being here," I said sincerely. "I had a great time."

"Me too, it was super fun." Then Temple asked, "Who is the next captain?"

"Scott Gravatt. And Jeff Hawe is coming along now, too," I said.

"The snowboard photographer?" Temple asked.

I told Temple how I'd met Jeff when he was taking photos for a magazine at Mount Bachelor during the Dirksen Derby the prior December. Jeff and I had got to talking about adventure and trips, and I'd told him about the trip I was putting together to pedal the whole West Coast. Jeff had grown up in Colorado, studied photography at college in Montana, and was currently living in Georgetown, a neighborhood of Seattle. We stayed in touch throughout the winter, and in the spring he told me he'd like to come along and take photos.

Next spread: We presented at many high schools along the way. Oxnard High School, California. 2013. *Jeff Hawe*

ikes, Boards, Blind
75 day tandem bicycle adventure, self-
pported and towing surfboards. A
laboration between friends and family to help
isually impaired athlete realize another
venture. A surf trip down the entire west
ast...began September 6, 2013.

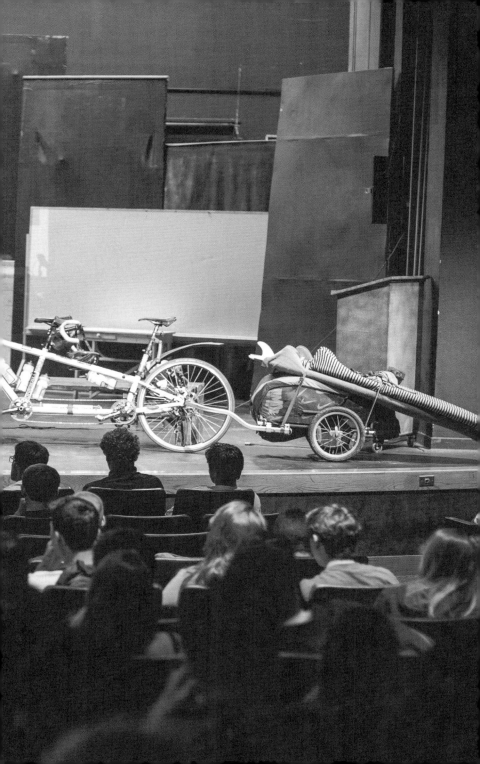

"Sweet," Temple said. "What is he going to do with them?"

"I'm not sure, but I know we'll use some of them on the blog. I think he is really just stoked on the trip. If he can make any money with his photos and the story, great. If not, then at least he cycled down the West Coast."

Barrett, Cannon, and Ayla came out to the truck and said their good-byes as well. Rebecca, Madrona, and I stood there waving as they pulled away. "Are you sad to see him go?" Rebecca asked.

"Yup. We always have a good time, and the last ten days were memorable." She put her arm around my shoulders and we all went inside to wait for Scott and Jeff.

Jeff arrived at the condo first. I gave him a hug and we sat down to catch up. "Have you been on any cool trips since I saw you in December?" I asked.

He told me about a trip to Alaska the previous April. "It was intense," he said. "I was shooting snowboard photos from a helicopter, and more than once I had to hang my body out of the chopper to get the shot."

"Wow," I said.

"It was an amazing trip, though, and I got some great photos."

"Well, I don't think you will have to do anything gnarly like that on this trip," I said. "Maybe just hang off your bike a little."

Jeff laughed. "Yeah, but let me show you this mounting bracket I've been working on." He went over to his pile of gear and pulled out a small metal arm roughly ten inches in length. "I can mount this thing on the forward part of my bike frame down around the height of my knees. I put my camera on this other end and then I run a trigger up to my handlebars. I can shoot all day and never stop pedaling," he finished. I knew he was smiling with pride.

Scott Gravatt, my roommate from college, showed up a few hours later. His daughter A.J. drove him out from Portland, and it was nice to see her for a brief second. I introduced Scott to Jeff and we all started helping out with dinner.

In the morning I started to put the bike, trailer, panniers, and surf gear back together in an organized fashion. I showed Scott which pannier was his and how to take the bag on and off its bracket. "Where is your surfboard?"

"It's outside in the grass," he replied matter-of-factly.

"You left it out all night?" I asked in astonishment.

"Dude, it's just a surfboard. It's fine." He went out and grabbed the board.

"I like your style," I said.

I lifted my pannier and clipped it on. Then I picked up Scott's. His bag felt super light. I opened it and started feeling through his clothing. "Dev, what are you doing?" Scott said with a huge laugh.

Jeff, laughing too, said, "He's going through your stuff, man."

"I am looking to see what you brought," I said to Scott. "I don't want you to get cold. You're not in Florida anymore." We were all laughing. Scott had lived in Portland for almost two years working for Nike, but he had been born and raised on the beaches of Florida. He was an ultramarathoner and great longboard surfer, but Jeff and I were not going to let him forget that he was in the Pacific Northwest now. I'd been in Washington for nearly twenty years, and Rebecca's uncles were still calling me a California guy. I wasn't going to miss my chance to haze the transplant. "Do you have any long johns or anything wool?" I asked.

"No," Scott replied defiantly.

"You don't even have any wool socks?"

"Nope," he said proudly. "I have this Nike track jacket, though." Jeff laughed again.

"What else?" I demanded.

"I have these brand-new bike shoes like you suggested," and Scott pulled out a shoe box that still had the tissue in it.

"You haven't even worn those yet?" I asked in mock horror.

"Nope," Scott said.

"Great, I'll find some Band-Aids and keep them in my pocket."

"Dev, relax, I'm not afraid of blisters."

"It's not you I'm worried about," I said. "I don't want to sit in the backseat and listen to you bitch all day."

It was gray and drizzly as we pedaled south out of Westport toward the Oregon border. Scott and I settled into a rhythm and Jeff found his own cadence as he trailed behind us.

In the evening we slept on the concrete pad of a public park's basketball court in a small town I had never heard of. "This place

Next spread: As we near the bridge over the Columbia River that will take us into Oregon, we pass through an eclectic landscape. Washington. 2013. *Jeff Hawe*

is a little sketchy," said Scott. "I keep expecting to see a motor home pull up, park, and then cook a batch."

"It's a little more than rural," I agreed.

"It's just the woods," Jeff said. "You're not in Florida anymore, Gravatt."

In the morning we woke to find that one of the trailer tires had gone flat. Scott changed the tube and pumped it up with a CO_2 cartridge. It took him only minutes. "I'm impressed, Gravatt. We might let you become a Northwesterner after all," I said.

In the early afternoon we approached the bridge that connects Longview to Astoria. It spans the Columbia River mouth and marks the state line between Washington and Oregon. "I'm stopping!" Scott shouted, using the captain's command. "This is gnarly," Scott said. "There is no bike lane and no shoulder. The lanes are super narrow and there are metal grates everywhere. How long is this bridge, Dev?"

I told him I didn't know and reminded him that he was the one with the iPhone. "Good point." He reached into the back pocket of his track jacket and pulled out his phone. "This bridge is four miles long, and it boasts the longest continuous truss in the nation—1,232 feet."

"Wow, you've really made this an educational moment," I replied.

"You're such a smart-ass," he said. "Do you have anything valuable to add to our conversation?"

"Actually, I do. Since the traffic is usually light this time of day, I suggest we start pedaling."

We pulled onto the bridge deck and began climbing at a slow click. Cars flew by and someone honked. "Damn," Scott said.

"Maybe they were stoked on our setup," I replied.

"I don't think so. Nobody is giving us an inch."

As we crawled along, I tried to think of something positive to say. "At least you and I can talk to each other!" I shouted over the traffic noise. "Poor Jeff is back there by himself."

"I forgot about Jeff!" Scott shouted back. "I should check to see if he's still alive." Scott turned his head to the left and looked over his shoulder. As he did, we drifted into the lane.

"Whoa, Bud! Jeff is still alive, but you're going to kill us by swerving into oncoming traffic," I teased. Soon we crested the apex of the bridge and began coasting downhill to the other side.

We relaxed as we cruised off the bridge, got back on Highway 101, and headed south. By late afternoon we pulled into Seaside and checked the waves in the cove at the south end of town. We booked a room at a motel right there on the sand in front of the surf spot and threw our stuff in the room.

"I'm going surfing," I said.

Jeff said he'd go too, and I asked Scott if he was coming along. "I think I'm going to borrow Jeff's camera and take photos of you guys from that rock wall over there. Is that alright with you, Jeff?

"Sure," Jeff replied, showing Scott the camera's features. "Don't drop it."

Jeff and I paddled out and caught some waves. Scott got a few nice photos of the evening's surf session, we ate a quick dinner, and then we headed to bed.

I awoke in the middle of the night to the sound of an iPhone ping. Then a phone rang, and I heard Scott talking to his daughter A.J. "Is everything alright?" I asked him when he got off the call.

"No," he said. "Our dog ate a bunch of rat poison and A.J. had to take him to the vet. She is there now and it doesn't sound good. I'm waiting to talk with the on-call veterinarian. Go back to sleep. I'll wake you up if I hear more."

An hour or so later I heard his phone ring again, and then heard Scott gathering up his gear.

"What did they say?" I asked.

"The dog died," Scott said flatly. "A.J. will be here in an hour or so to pick me up."

"Are you coming back?"

"I don't think so, Dev. My kid is pretty shook up and Denise is out of town. I'm super sorry, but I think I'm out."

Jeff and I said good-bye to Scott and decided to wait until morning to figure things out.

We got up early and I made some coffee. Then we began transferring Jeff's gear into the trailer and panniers on the tandem. We locked Jeff's bike to a post under the carport of the motel and left the key with the receptionist. "I will find someone to pick your bike up and bring it down to Pacific City," I said. The Oregon beach town was our next captain swap-out spot. Then we climbed aboard and kept pushing south, enjoying playful waves and total sun for the next three days. We took our time. Jeff got some great photos of pristine Oregon beaches, and he put them up on the blog from a bakery in Manzanita, a beach town along the way.

In the late afternoon of the third day, Jeff and I cycled into Pacific City. We pulled up to the beach, leaned the bike on a post, and sat in the sand. I could tell Jeff was sore.

"I'm sorry, man," I said. "I think you might be too tall for the tandem. Do your knees hurt?"

"A little," Jeff said. "It has just a slightly different pedal motion than my bike." We sat there, facing the ocean. "The waves are huge right now," Jeff said.

"They sound big," I said. "And it's forecasted to continue building all week."

The following day came together flawlessly. Rebecca showed up with Jeff's bike, and the next captain, Tom Herron, showed up with his wife, Verna. He was ready to pedal and his stoke for cycling was the breath of fresh air we needed.

"Jeff, this is Dr. Tom Herron, the man who I began riding on the tandem bike with," I said. Tom laughed that I called him a doctor, and then introduced Jeff to Verna.

The next morning Rebecca and Verna drove off. Jeff packed the remainder of his clothes back into his own panniers. "Becca saved the day," Jeff said. "I've got to do something special for her. She is amazing."

"For sure. She's running the show from behind the scenes, and that's why it's all going so smoothly," I agreed.

I climbed onto the tandem behind Tom. "Alright, Devon," he said, "are we ready?"

"Ready," I replied to his customary captain's command, and we started pedaling in unison. Soon the coastal drizzle turned to rain, and then it began to rain hard. Not long after that it began to pour, and then it started to pelt. "This may be the most wet I have ever been on a bicycle!" Tom shouted with excitement.

Tom asked how far it was to the next town. "We hit Lincoln City in thirty miles," I said. He suggested that we stop for a coffee—but maybe it was a demand.

When we arrived in Lincoln City we grabbed more than a coffee. We got a motel room as well. Tom stepped off the bike and

I remained standing over my seat. "Are you alright, Devon?" the doctor asked.

"I'm fine. I'm just waiting for the water to drain out of my ears."

In the morning we put our wet gear back on and started pedaling again.

Not long into our ride, I heard a car slow down as it prepared to pass us. "Dude, the guy in the back is not pedaling!" someone shouted out the window." Tom laughed, knowing full well that it was impossible for me to not be pedaling while he was because the cranks were connected. Plus, he could feel me pushing. We were an easy target and these tandem-themed jokes came often. "Rainbow love!" shouted some young guys. "There's a guy right behind you, chasing you!" called out others. Soon, I decided to start jotting them down in our trip journal, alongside other random data, like the number of cheeseburgers we'd eaten, disk brake pads we'd gone through, lattes we'd drunk, and flat tires we'd repaired.

The rain was relentless for three more days, and the surf was gigantic. Surprisingly, though, it was not an unruly, washing-machine mess. The ominous, dark faces remained smooth, and the waves had a beautiful peel. One of the photos Jeff took on that stretch ended up as a two-page spread about the trip in *Surfer* magazine, and another one ended up on a T-shirt for a major surf brand. As Tom checked us into another roadside motel, Jeff and I complained about the sheer amount of rain we were encountering. "I just want to start one morning with dry clothes," Jeff said.

"You never know," I said. "Maybe our room will have a heater this time." The three of us headed to our room, Tom opened the door, and we all got a whiff of the stench. "Smells like cat piss," I said. "My bivy sack had a similar odor at the beginning of the trip."

"How did you get rid of the smell?" Tom asked with a note of hope.

"I threw it in the dumpster."

Jeff started hanging his wet clothing from a chair he had positioned in front of the room's only wall heater. Tom started stuffing his shoes with newspaper. "What do you have going on there?" I asked. When the good doctor explained that newspaper pulls the moisture out, Jeff and I began stuffing newspaper into our shoes.

I took the lampshade off the table lamp and hung my wool undershirt over the bulb. "What do you have going on there, Devon?" Tom asked with a laugh.

"This bulb is an incandescent bulb, not an LED one. It produces heat," I responded, attempting the same tone of casual wisdom that Tom used when explaining his newspaper trick. "You watch: My shirt will be dry in the morning."

"Or at least a small circle of it will be," Jeff scoffed.

In the morning we headed to the banquet room to feast on the complimentary continental breakfast buffet. I ate a banana that I am sure was previously frozen and two spoonsful of Skippy peanut butter that I dug from the bottom of the jar.

We climbed back onto the bike. "You know, guys," I said, "I actually got a nice night's sleep. I think Cat Piss Motel has some of the best mattresses so far."

"I slept pretty good, too," Jeff said. "And at least half of my clothes are dry."

As we pulled into Humbug Mountain State Park and set up camp, the sun was starting to set. Jeff and I grabbed our boards and ran out to the beach. "It looks small and sloppy," Jeff said.

"Whatever," I replied. "Let's go surfing."

We got out of the water after dark and walked back to find Tom. "It felt so good to be in the water," I said. The three of us enjoyed a gourmet camp dinner and sat for hours around the table, talking about everything and nothing at all.

Each day was an exercise in repetition. We woke up, packed the bike trailer, turned our socks inside out, and pedaled south. My body had grown accustomed to the routine, and I felt genuinely good in the mornings despite the fact that my bike shorts had been soaking wet for the past 300 miles.

As we cycled into Crescent City, California, we said hello to our good friend the rain again. Then we said hello to rain's friend, wind, and things began to get blustery. "I think it's time for another motel," Tom said, and we found one on the highway near downtown. Tom checked us in while Jeff and I waited in the lobby.

"Oh man," Jeff said. "You gotta hear this. The hotel staff has plastered the place with NOAA warnings forecasting the worst storm in a hundred years to hit Crescent City sometime late tonight."

"Nice," I said. "Maybe we should go surfing."

"It's blowing like forty miles per hour out there," Jeff said with skepticism.

I told him about a guy from the local Surfrider Foundation, Walter, I'd traded e-mails with, and said I could ask him to suggest a place to get some surf. I dialed Walter's number and he picked up on the second ring. He said he and his family had been following our trip on the blog and asked if we wanted to go surfing. "Of course," I said. "It's pretty windy out there, though." Walter said he knew a place where the wind was blowing offshore and offered to pick us up.

Tom hung back at the motel. Jeff and I promised him we would be safe, loaded into Walter's truck, and drove to his secret beach. He definitely knew his spot. The wind was still howling, but it was blowing right into the wave faces. "It looks big," Jeff said.

"It's not as big as it looks," Walter said, explaining that the wind was making the wave faces stand up. They also sounded like they were slow to break; the wind was doing that too. The three of us paddled out and tried to stay close to each other. Walter caught a few waves right off. A set came through and I stroked hard, but the wind blew me back off the lip and I couldn't get into the wave. The same thing happened to Walter on the next one.

"I'm having a tough time reading them," I said to Walter. "My eyes can't see any contrast with all this wind ripple." Walter said he would tell me when a good one was coming. It didn't take long. The sides of my eyes saw the dark shape lumbering in and then it got darker as it grew nearer.

"Go now!" Walter shouted, and I turned and dropped. I slid into a steep slow pocket and started pumping as hard as I could. It was tough to keep my surfboard on the face of the wave because the wind was trying to blow me backward. I set my backside rail and dug in for a heel carve as I went up the wave and tried to hit the lip. The wind blew me out and my ride was over.

We spent some time recounting waves back on the sand, then Walter dropped us off. In the morning I expected to wake up to a power outage and a flood in the streets, but things were normal. The three of us went out to the lobby for our morning motel coffee and then began packing up again.

"I did a little research on average annual rainfalls," Jeff said. "You guys might want to take a seat for this." Jeff told us that while the average rainfall on the coast of Oregon for the month of September is 3.2 inches, that September of 2013 it had received just over ten inches. "This past month has been the wettest on record since they began keeping track," he said.

When we got on the bike, Tom was still laughing about the ridiculous conditions we had gone through. In the afternoon we entered California's fabled redwood forest. The following day we pedaled past gigantic redwood trees. In the afternoon we veered west and climbed over the mountains toward the Pacific Ocean. As the afternoon began to melt into dusk, we crested our last hill and began coasting down. "I can see the ocean," Tom said. Soon we were on the legendary Pacific Coast Highway. Just before dark, we pulled into our campsite at Fort Bragg.

The three of us went through the familiar routine of unpacking, then sat around a picnic table for a team planning meeting. We were three days ahead of schedule, something I attributed to the bad weather forcing us to skip our daily surf sessions and Jeff admiringly chalked up to Tom's maniac cycling pace. Tom pointed out that we'd pedaled just over a hundred miles that day. It was the first and would also be the last day I cycled a hundred miles on the trip. Most of the daily mileage had been fifty to sixty miles. It was a nice feeling to get a hundred-mile day in and I sat at the table silent and grateful for Tom Herron's passion, not only for cycling, but people, too.

"Forty-five miles south is a famous surf spot called Point Arena," I said. "I suggest we head there in the morning. If we get waves, then we could stay a few nights and keep surfing. Then it's a quick pedal to Bodega Bay." Rebecca had rented a house for us for two nights in Bodega Bay and planned to fly down with my sister to say hello.

The next day, Tom steered the bike into the parking lot at the foot of the small cove at Point Arena and looked for a spot to view the waves. I could sense that swell was hitting the point and the waves were good—or maybe I just sensed how crowded the parking lot was and heard some surfers talking with excitement. Jeff and I spent the next two days surfing perfect waves at the point.

We found the rental house in Bodega Bay and leaned the tandem bike against the outside of the garage door. As we dismounted, I said to Tom, "You have brought me along for over six hundred miles, the longest leg of any captain. Thank you."

"It's been the trip of a lifetime, Devon," Tom said.

The day turned to night and I heard the doorbell ring. Rebecca, my sister Laura, and Mike Cummins, Temple's older brother—and the leg's next captain—were at the door. It felt good to hold Rebecca in my arms. Tom's wife Verna had shown up earlier with their Suburban, ready to make the fifteen-hour drive back to Washington with her husband.

I had one more day and one more night with Rebecca, so we made the best of it. The five of us piled into her rental car and drove fifteen miles north to Salmon Creek Beach. Mike and I went surfing while Becca and Laura sat in the sun. In the evening we went to dinner with my Aunt Cynthy and Uncle Norman, who drove over from Sonoma to meet us. They picked up the tab for dinner. Back at the rental house, I started showing Mike how everything goes together on the bike rig.

The morning came too quickly, and it was hard to say goodbye to Rebecca. I had almost everything packed onto the bike, and she and I stood in front of the house while we waited for Mike. Then I heard the front door open and Becca giggle. When I asked what was so funny, Rebecca said, "Mike is wearing a long-sleeve, button-up denim shirt and a skateboard helmet."

I made a few cowboy jokes, and Mike and I pedaled off slowly, very slowly. "What's the matter?" I asked. "We are going to fall over."

"I don't think I'm in the right gear," Mike said as he stared down at the sprockets.

"Okay, let's stop and figure it out," I said. "Are the girls looking at us?"

Mike looked over his shoulder and back down the driveway. "Yup," he said. "It's alright!" he shouted. "Just working out the kinks."

We continued working out the kinks for the remainder of the day, constantly swerving, losing a chain, and laughing the whole time. When the sun was directly overhead, Mike said he was hot. "Maybe you should give Willie Nelson his shirt back," I said.

Next spread: Cowboy TV has us all entranced on the Point Arena beach. California. 2013. *Jeff Hawe*

"Maybe you should give Stevie Wonder his sunglasses back," Mike countered.

"Devon, towing the trailer is a new thing for me," Mike said. "Going uphill is like towing a dirty wet stump and going downhill is like being pushed by a rhinoceros."

That night we slept in Inverness, and we went surfing nearby in the morning. Then we got back on the bike and found our pedaling rhythm had improved drastically. Mike is a great athlete. He rips at skating, surfing, and snowboarding, and he figured things out quickly. We continued to get in sync, and by the afternoon we had made it all the way to the Golden Gate Bridge. Mike pulled into the parking lot on the north end, and we got off the tandem to take a look at the gigantic landmark before we crossed.

After crossing, it took an hour to get through downtown San Francisco. We found a motel on the south end of the city, directly across from Ocean Beach. Mike and I went surfing while Jeff met up with some friends. Walking back through the sand at sunset, I said, "Those waves reminded me of Oregon surf."

"You mean shifty with juice," Mike laughed.

The following day we got back on the coast highway toward Santa Cruz and pulled off to check every surf spot we knew of. In the afternoon we surfed Waddell Creek, where we all agreed the waves seemed the most promising. We spotted a flat, grassy field on the hill across the highway that looked like a good place to spend the night. We set up camp in the field and sat at a picnic table for sunset and our planning meeting. "Tom Burt is driving down from Tahoe tomorrow night and we are going to meet him at his friend Gus's house in Santa Cruz," I explained. Tom would take Mike to the airport before starting his leg as captain.

We drank our coffee slowly in the morning. Mike and Jeff could see the waves across the highway and the decision was made to wait and surf in Santa Cruz, where we hoped the swell would be cleaner.

It was easy to find Gus's house; he was just a block off the bike path in Capitola. I knocked on the door and then gave him a hug

Opposite: Mike Cummins and I push the tandem bike up a steep driveway. Jeff Hawe follows behind. Bodega Bay, California. 2013. Rebecca Raney

like we were old friends. Tom Burt arrived after dinner and just walked through the front door carrying a pie. "What's up, Raney?" he said. "I made you an apple pie with apples I pulled from a tree at the post office near my house."

"Nice, Burt, you're a twenty-first-century hobo," I laughed.

In the morning, Gus put together a bunch of longboards and we all piled into his minivan. We surfed at the top of Pleasure Point. I was like a little kid in a candy store, paddling all over the place with spastic energy. It was great being back on a longboard, and I caught some zippers. For the first two years after my eye diagnosis, I primarily rode my longboard to build confidence during a time when everything felt off. After the surf we said good-bye to Mike.

"Are we ready?" Tom asked the following morning. I was surprised to notice he was wearing flip-flops and asked if he owned some clip-in shoes. "Raney, I've never pedaled more than twenty miles on a road bike before," he replied.

"Well, today is going to be twice as long, Burt," I said, and off we went, laughing. The highway was flat for most of the morning and I didn't notice the flip-flops at all. Tom is a gifted athlete and our rhythm fell into sync almost immediately, just like when I'm behind him on a snowboard.

After we'd been pedaling for a while, Tom asked how the trip had been going. "Ah, Burt, if I could figure a way to tow my family along I could do this for the rest of my life," I answered. "It's been amazing. I exercise all day. I surf almost every day. I hang out with my buddies, laughing all day. I visit new beaches and towns. And everyone involved seems to be having just as much fun as I am."

We stayed two nights in Carmel with Chris and Bev Sanders, some more friends of Tom's, and surfed in the cove at the base of town. As we were leaving, Chris said, "I made you guys some stickers. They say B3, for BikesBoardsBlind," and he handed Tom a pile.

"These are rad," Jeff said as he slapped a few on his bike as well as the tandem. I thanked him, and then we pushed off for Big Sur.

On the outskirts of Carmel, Tom steered the bike into the parking lot of a Safeway. I held the tandem while he went in for some snacks. He came out with a gallon of water and a rotisserie chicken. I burst out laughing. "Dude, that chicken is a quarter the size of the entire bike trailer," I said.

"Keep laughing, Raney," he said. "When your almonds are gone you're going to be begging me for some of this bird."

We would spend the next five days cycling on the Big Sur highway, surfing perfect head-high waves, and sleeping wherever we found a flat piece of dirt. On our third morning I woke up hungry. "It's here somewhere!" I said as I rifled through our bike trailer searching for the bagel I had been saving. Most of our gear lay in the dirt, without order, as we had begun to pack up. "Found it!" I exclaimed as I held up my bagel. "Oh yeah, I won't be eating an oatmeal packet for breakfast today, dudes!" I said to Tom and Jeff. "I just have to brush off the sand." Brushing the dirt off my bagel, I felt some pieces missing, or rather some nibbles. Showing it to Tom Burt, I asked, "Did a mouse eat my bagel?"

He looked, laughed, and replied, "Yup, a mouse has been loving your bagel."

"Damn it," I said, "I am starving." Grabbing the bagel, Tom cut the top off and handed it back to me. Now I was laughing. "I didn't pedal fourteen hundred miles to get the frickin' hantavirus, Burt."

"Don't be a sissy, Raney, just eat your bagel."

"I guess I'll have to eat this bagel, Burt, since our only other food is what's left of that bony chicken carcass you picked up three days ago." All three of us were in hysterics. "That damn carcass has been baking in the ninety-degree heat for days."

Unable to stop laughing, Tom replied, "How do you think they cooked it, Raney? It was baking when we bought it."

We pedaled up out of the valley and back onto the coast highway. We climbed and coasted for a few hours as the road rose and fell while running parallel with the Pacific Ocean. "We should be coming up on Fuller's soon," Tom said. Fuller's is a left-hand, open-ocean point wave that breaks on boulders. It's a hardly-spoken-of legend, and the regular crews who call it theirs have done a great job of keeping it private.

Tom had only surfed it once. "I might not recognize the trail," he said, and I agreed that it wouldn't be marked. We cycled on for

Next spread: Looking for a bottom turn at Sand Dollar Beach. Big Sur, California. 2013. *Jeff Hawe*

a while and then Tom pulled off to the right side of the highway, hopped off the bike, and disappeared down the bank. In a few minutes he returned. "Let's go," he said, and we began unpacking the trailer so we could get to our wetsuits. Tom disappeared into the brush again and quickly returned with a stick.

"What's that?" I asked.

"It's your walking stick," he replied. "I'm guessing the trail takes us down seven hundred feet of vertical, and I think they keep it sketchy on purpose." He told me to put on my bike helmet, using his grown-up voice for the first time. "You didn't pedal fourteen hundred miles to get the hantavirus, Raney, and you didn't pedal this far to splatter your brains on the rocks, either."

The three of us began descending the trail and left everything but our surf gear up on the highway unlocked. I began to sweat as I tried to feel my way downhill. Soon I was holding Tom's hand. My body was tense throughout the descent, and I think I burned more calories walking down that trail than I did cycling all day. We hit the sand at the base of the trail and put our wetsuits on.

"The waves are clean, maybe shoulder-high, and peeling," Tom told me enthusiastically. "And there's only one guy out. There is one issue, though. There is big-ass rock in front of the takeoff."

I heard the alarm in his voice. "How big?" I asked.

"It's hard to tell, but the dry section looks as big as a VW Bug. Here comes a set—let's watch for a second." We were silent for a bit, and then Tom gave his assessment. "Those ones were head high. The rock isn't an issue if you take off in the right spot because then it's behind you by the time you're surfing. We will just have to sit out there for a bit and find the spot."

"I'm going to take a few photos of you guys, and then I'll meet you in the water," Jeff said.

We paddled out. Tom and I gave the local guy a respectful amount of space as we sat out on the shoulder. We watched him catch every wave he wanted. Then we paddled a little deeper toward the takeoff spot. It wasn't long before Tom caught a wave and then took another. I missed every one he told me to go for. I couldn't seem to find the right spot on the wave with enough energy to throw me into the pocket. I needed to be deeper, and soon I was sitting near the local.

I was having a frustrating time. Tom paddled over and began talking with the other surfer. The guy caught another wave and Tom came back over my way. I asked what they were talking about. "I said hello, and he was super friendly, so I told him that you're blind." When I expressed my shock, he said, "You need to just let people know how bad your eyes are, D. You'll feel more relaxed and they might even help you out."

As the surfer paddled back out from his last ride, he shouted, "Come sit over here!" I followed him. "I'll tell you when to go," he said, and we waited silently. A few set waves rolled through and he remained silent. The sides of my eyes picked up the last wave of the set, growing darker as it got nearer. "Go on this one!" he shouted. "Go now." I spun around and slid my board under my feet and slipped right into the pocket. The wave was curling and reeling with speed. I did a couple of heel-side speed pumps to get out front on the face, and then I set my rail and went up the wall. I hit the lip and put all I had into my backside cutback. I wanted my crew to be proud.

I paddled back out and enthusiastically thanked the guy, my gratitude obvious by the size of my grin. We kept surfing until the tide dropped out, and then we hiked up the trail.

It was well past dark when we found a place to sleep that night. The following day we surfed perfect waves again and that night slept under a giant oak tree that stood alone in a riverbed. On the morning after that, we enjoyed more perfect surf at that dry riverbed's mouth. Then we left Big Sur and rode into Morro Bay in the afternoon. It was only then that the swell finally died. It showed up the day Tom Burt arrived at Gus's and quit one day before he was leaving.

We found a campsite in Morro Bay and hung our wetsuits on a tree limb to dry in the late sun. The three of us sat down at the picnic bench and had our planning meeting. "Who is the next captain?" Tom asked. I told him Ron Hendrickson was flying into San Luis Obispo the next evening and taking a cab to the motel Rebecca picked out.

Next spread: Tom Burt and me suiting up. We slept under this tree for two nights and surfed great waves out front. Big Sur, California. 2013. *Jeff Hawe*

The next day I walked with Tom to the Greyhound station in San Luis Obispo, where he would take a bus back to Gus's in Santa Cruz and pick up his car. "It was pretty awesome when that local surfer called you into your first wave at Fuller's," he said. "Don't be afraid to let people know how bad your eyes really are, Raney."

"You're a good man, Burt," I said. "Thank you for being here. I'll be thinking about the past nine days for a long time." Tom gave me a hug and then got on the bus.

Ron Hendrickson showed up at the motel that evening. I introduced my former boss to Jeff and we all went through the routine of catching up. "Show me where to put my gear and I'll pack up the bike," Ron said. When I told him we had been putting the rig together in the mornings, he put on the boss voice I knew so well. "Just show me where my stuff goes."

I laughed. "We don't have a firm a.m. start time," I teased. "We just roll whenever."

"Oh, Devon, you know I like a detailed schedule," he replied.

"I know. I'm glad you're here, man," I said with sincere appreciation.

Ron had been a mentor to me for a long time. He taught me everything I know about building houses. He taught me a good deal about life as well, and I was stoked to be sitting behind him as we pedaled along the coast the following morning, through Pismo Beach.

Ron found a rural back road on his iPhone that ran into Lompoc. "It looks fun, and we'll have a nice hill to climb," he said. His detour proved to be a good choice, and we pedaled along without traffic as I told Ron some funny stories from the past few weeks. It had been a while since we encountered any traffic at all, but eventually I heard a car slow its engine as it approached and prepared to pass us. After nearly two months of hearing random people yell their favorite tandem jokes, I figured in a second I would hear a guy shout to Ron that I was sitting in the back with my legs up, smoking a cigar and watching a movie. Instead, at the last second the vehicle sped up and passed us closely while the passenger blew an airhorn out the window. In an instant Ron threw out his middle finger and shouted, "Asshole!"

I laughed and said, "You definitely don't have a problem asserting yourself. That was the first middle finger of the trip."

"I'm glad I can be the first at something on this trip," Ron said with a laugh.

We spent the night at a campground in Lompoc and Ron asked where we were headed the next day. "Out to Jalama Beach," I replied. "You are going to love it. It's one of my favorite places to surf." I told Ron that we might spend one or two nights at Jalama, depending on the surf. He pretended to grouse about the loose schedule and we all turned in for the night, chuckling.

We got up the next morning, ate breakfast at a greasy spoon, and then pedaled out toward the ocean. We climbed the steep road toward Jalama and when we reached the bluff at the top, Jeff pulled his bike up alongside us. "The waves look insane," he said. "It's big, too."

Ron brought the tandem bike to a stop in front of the ranger's booth at the entrance to the campground. I asked whether any beachfront sites were still available; the ranger replied there was just one left. I told him we'd take it for two nights and asked the ranger what the swell was doing. "It's out of the northwest and measuring four feet at twenty-two seconds," he replied as he handed over our receipt.

"Oh my God," I mumbled as we pulled away.

"That must be a pretty good report," Ron said.

"It's the royal flush of surf reports for this spot," I replied.

The waves did not disappoint. Jeff and I surfed clean, organized, and generously spaced-out peelers with gigantic faces for two days and on the morning of the third day as well.

In the late morning, Ron and I packed up and Jeff scrolled through his camera. "Devon, I got some nice shots of you dropping in on some good-sized rights," he said.

"Awesome. I wish I could see them. Let's get on the bikes," I replied.

Sometimes Jeff got annoyed with my constant need to be doing something; this was probably one of those moments. Jeff is patient, methodical, and takes his time. Usually the two of us were a nice complement to each other. But fifty days on the road together

Next spread: I take a lot of falls, but sometimes magic happens: on this one I took off deep and everything fell into place. Jalama Beach, California. 2013. *Jeff Hawe*

can wear a person thin, and sometimes I could sense my energy was causing friction. Yet months after the trip was over, I realized I'd ended up developing a deep and lasting friendship with Jeff.

Soon we were all pedaling back up onto the bluff and headed south. As Ron and I crested over the top of the most recent uphill climb, we started coasting. "Let's pedal super hard!" I shouted.

"It's steep, curvy, and the road has some gravel!" Ron shouted back. I assured him the bike would hold and soon we were hauling ass. The road flattened out and we reconnected with the 101 south. It was early afternoon when we pulled into Refugio State Park and set up camp.

"Thank you for patiently hanging out in Jalama while we went surfing this whole time," I said. "It was probably not as much fun for you."

"The beach was beautiful and I enjoyed watching you guys," Ron said. "I heard other surfers say it was double overhead out there, but I know all you guys lie a little," he teased. "Then I realized the waves were really big." I was glad he was there to see it.

Ron bought some wood, and the three of us sat around the fire and had our planning meeting. I told them that my brother, Blake, would meet us in Carpinteria the following night and would be captaining the last leg of the trip. Ron said his family would be flying in, and they would be staying a few days at a vacation home Rebecca had recommended.

Family was the theme of the evening, and I talked about how I wanted to use our float day to visit my grandparents. I also planned to use that day to spend time with Rebecca and Madrona, who had driven the truck down. It had been two weeks since I'd seen Rebecca in Bodega Bay and a full month since I'd seen my daughter.

In the morning we did the usual, except this time I kept my flip phone on me so I could call my grandma to see the best time for me to come over. We left the highway for a bike path once we entered Goleta.

Just southeast of Goleta, Ron said he could see a fruit stand up ahead. "Let's stop," I said. "I would love some strawberries." I stood over the bike and held the rig while Ron bought two containers and Jeff grabbed some other fruit for himself. I was halfway through my box when my phone rang.

It was my father. "Hey Dad, how's it going?" I asked.

"Devon, your grandpa passed away in his sleep this morning."

"I'm really sorry, Dad. How are you doing?" We spoke for a while about how my grandma was doing and the funeral arrangements that were already underway. "I will see you in a few days, then," I said as I hung up the phone.

Back on the tandem, Ron asked how I was feeling. "I'm good," I said. "My grandpa was ninety-eight years old, lived a stand-up life, and died in his sleep. He had a sharp mind until the end and I really don't feel that sad. It does feel strange to miss him by only a day, though."

Rebecca and Madrona were at the rental house in Carpinteria when we pulled up that evening. I kissed Rebecca and held my daughter for a long time. Blake showed up later that night. A family decision was made to wait two extra days before we started the ride again. My parents flew in to help with funeral arrangements, and it was nice to say hello to them both. My dad seemed to be doing well and was beginning to write his words for the service. I spent as much time as possible at Madrona's side, walking hand in hand to the beach as I shared stories from the adventure so far.

The time came to leave, and Blake took the reins as the adventure's last captain, the anchor of the trip. I sat behind my brother and pedaled south along the bluff trail in Carpinteria. "I'm super glad you're here, Blake," I said. My brother has three kids, a daughter and two boys, all at different grade levels and all going to separate schools—it's busy at Blake's house. It was a big deal for him to leave for more than a week.

"I wouldn't miss it," Blake said. "I don't know if I told you, but I got a new road bike a while back and have been trying to not drive if I can pedal instead."

"I thought your thighs looked huge," I said, and the jokes that had been part of every leg of the adventure began again.

We connected with the 101 South and soon were passing the legendary Rincon Point. "They call this spot the Queen of the Coast," I told Blake as I shared my excitement.

Next spread: I could spend a lifetime on the beach with my family. Carpinteria, California. 2013. *Jeff Hawe*

"I know," he said flatly, and I tried to remind myself not to be such a big brother. As we passed Rincon, Blake noted the complete absence of surfers. That was a bad sign. Even without a hint of swell someone would be out in the water at Rincon, sitting on their board and watching the sunset or maybe checking their iPhone. I started to get bummed, because I knew this lack of swell at Rincon meant it was going to be tough to find a wave at my favorite spots in Ventura. In fifteen miles I would know for sure.

We exited the 101 and pedaled on the flat beachfront PCH that held so many memories for me. I shouted to Blake excitedly every time we passed a campground or surf spot I thought he might remember. I had been coming back to the area a couple of times a year for nearly twenty years. For the past five years, Rebecca and I had spent the month of October on that stretch of beach as I introduced Madrona to some special sandy places that will stay in my memory always. Blake had not come back nearly as much. He had moved to Washington at the start of his freshman year in high school and considers Washington to be where he grew up.

I kept trying to make a connection for Blake and the area. "Do you remember going to the Pirate Ship on the sand in the Ventura Harbor? We used to go there all the time. It's a super-good surf spot, right out in front at the rock jetties," I said, peppering him with my enthusiasm.

"I think I remember that," he responded with disinterest. "When do you want to eat?"

At the end of the road we pulled through a small ranger pay booth. Highway 101 ran above us and there were a number of cars parked beneath the overpass. The car owners were out surfing a deep-water bump called Overhead. As Jeff, Blake, and I stared out at the wave, I explained what I had been told by the older surfers when I was a kid. According to them, Overhead always has a wave—even when nearby places like Rincon are relatively flat. It picks up all hints of swell because a large pile of railroad boxcars was dropped on the ocean floor by the navy during World War II.

"Is this where we are surfing?" Jeff asked. "It looks like a long paddle."

"No," I replied. "I don't love it out there. It's a tight takeoff spot, which makes it more crowded than it looks, and although the drop is cool, the ride is over pretty much after that." I told

Jeff the spot I'd been bragging about for months was just down the road.

I had been rambling on to Jeff throughout the trip about a secret spot I called Road Washout. Of course, I knew full well there was nothing secret about it at all, and I wasn't even sure it was actually a surf spot, although I had surfed there many times with other surfers in the water. I had also never heard another surfer call the spot out by name, which is why I gave it one. The wave is located out front of some motor home–only campsites, which are really just asphalt parking pads angled toward the ocean. The asphalt runs for a couple of hundred yards or so and then disappears abruptly at the point where everything has washed away. The cobbles in front have been shifted around, and a right-hand point wave exists when the conditions are right. Like all the other points nearby, my little gem needs some northwest angle and some size. When it happens, the waves are super fun. The peel of the wave face is short and quick and has a little more punch than most point waves.

I stood with Jeff and Blake at the edge of Road Washout. "There is a wave, but it's closing out, and the low tide is showing exposed rocks," Jeff said. "There are two guys out, though."

I was slightly embarrassed that I had been bragging about this uncrowded gem and today it was a closeout with two guys on it. "I'm going surfing!" I shouted with stoke. "I love this place." Jeff and Blake took a pass. Secretly, I didn't want to surf there either, but I'd been talking about this place for two months and I'd be shamed if I didn't get in.

I wished we could have stayed in Ventura for a few days, but our extra days of float were used up already when we postponed our departure at the beginning of Blake's stint. So we kept moving south, across the Ventura–Los Angeles county line, and stayed at Leo Carrillo State Park. The next day we pedaled through the high-rent district of Malibu. Our day ended in Manhattan Beach, where the city truly came right up to the sand. We spent the night in a hotel there, since the affordable roadside motels seemed to have disappeared many miles back. "Tomorrow we're pedaling through Compton," I said.

"Oh yeah, gangstas' paradise," Blake noted, and we went to bed reciting our favorite rap lyrics, most of which were from the NWA song "Boyz-N-The Hood."

My phone rang in the morning. It was Scott Gravatt, the captain from leg two who had to pull out of the adventure. We hadn't talked in the two months since he'd left the trip. He was staying in Huntington Beach at the Hilton Waterfront Beach Resort for business, knew we were nearby since he'd been following the blog, and suggested we stay with him as we passed through.

In the afternoon I handed the bike off to a Hilton valet parking attendant, and then someone else with a bow tie brought our bags up to the room. Scott was on one of the top floors with a balcony, with two queen beds and a view of the Huntington Beach Pier. We stayed two nights instead of one.

The waves were good on a sand bar just south of the pier. In the morning and in the evening the wind was undetectable. Jeff took some great photos using his water housing, and Blake was enjoying being in the water as well.

It was dark outside on the morning of the second day when we said good-bye to Scott and got back on the road. Cycling away, I thought about how cool it was that he made it back on the adventure and that this time we were able to say our farewells on a solid note. It felt like everything on the trip worked itself out—that our karma was perfect.

Over the next two days we passed through iconic California beach towns like Laguna Beach, Dana Point, and San Clemente. We tried surfing at Salt Creek, but it was so crowded it felt dangerous.

We pulled into an oceanfront bluff site at San Elijo State Beach in Cardiff-by-the-Sea for our final night of the trip. The waves were small, but clean and defined at the point where they bumped up on the rock reef. It was sunny out and all three of us went surfing. In the evening we found some wood, built a fire, and sat around talking for as long as we could stay up.

We woke early to the Surfliner train's horn. We packed up the bike, walked across the street for donuts, and then pushed off for the remaining forty-five miles. Shortly after noon we arrived at the United States–Mexico border and rested the tandem bike on a signpost near the turnstile. It was crowded and busy, and a man tried to sell me a watch. He opened his trench coat and showed us the watches dangling for sale inside the garment. I was very grateful he was wearing jeans and a T-shirt as well, and that the outdated timepieces were in fact all he was showing us. "No, *gracias*," I said.

Jeff handed me a B3 sticker from the stack Chris Sanders had given us a month earlier. He took me over to a sign he had scouted and I slapped our stamp of proof just below the words "To Mexico."

My friend Vanessa, who I have known since middle school, drove down from her house in San Diego and met us in the parking lot. Her husband, Michael, brought his car as well, so we had two vehicles to load our bikes, boards, and gear into. They drove us back into San Diego and dropped us off at a time-share condo Rebecca's parents had secured. We pulled our bikes and gear from Vanessa and Michael's cars and agreed to meet up the following night. In the evening, Rebecca and Madrona drove into town with our truck. "Congratulations, you did it!" Becca said, and I could tell she was proud as she hugged me. I held Madrona tight. "Pretty cool, don't you think?" I asked. She just nodded and kept her arms around me.

The following night we did, in fact, party. Jeff put together a slide show from the images he'd captured throughout the journey, and we gave our presentation at Bird's Surf Shed in town. A keg and a taco cart were rented for the occasion. My parents, Rebecca's parents, and lots of friends showed up. All six captains—Blake was number seven—called me that evening to share their excitement that the adventure ended successfully. People we'd met along the way, people who'd shared their homes, and friends just stoked to see us finish called as well.

I said good-bye to Blake. "Thank you for being here, Brother. It would not have been the same without you." We knew we'd be meeting up again two days later for our grandfather's funeral, but I still wanted to formally thank him as captain.

Blake and Jeff made their respective travel plans and I loaded the gear into our truck. I put the tandem as well as Jeff's bike—which I would take back to Washington—on the rack. And Rebecca, Madrona, and I began driving back up the coast I had just spent seventy-two days pedaling down.

After a stop in Ventura for the memorial service—a happy time of reflection—we kept driving north. In Big Sur I got to share one of my favorite moments from the adventure: The three of us slept in the back of our truck in the dry riverbed under the lonesome and gigantic oak tree. A day later we stopped in Santa Cruz and stayed the night at Gus's house, and we got to meet Gus's wife, Cheryl. Just like I'd figured, everyone hit it off. We stayed two nights at the Burts' house in Kings Beach on the north shore of Lake Tahoe. Rebecca absolutely loved hearing Tom tell his favorite stories from the trip. With his electric energy, he shed light on all sorts of details I'd failed to mention. Tom's daughters Hannah and Nina laughed alongside Madrona as evening became night and we continued recalling our highlights. The best moment for me was when Tom's wife, Trish, said, "Devon, if you ever plan another tandem bicycle trip, it's my turn to be captain." It simply felt like everyone was connected in some way.

. Two weeks after I put our B3 sticker up at the border, I was back on Bainbridge Island. Madrona went back to school, and soon I found myself putting the bike rig back together one last time. Only this time Rebecca was the captain, and I was showing her how to clip the panniers on and how to strap the surfboards to the top of our trailer. We stuffed the bags with beach towels and filled the trailer with blankets to make the bike look fully loaded. We were heading to Madrona's elementary school to give her third-grade class our adventure talk.

The class had followed our progress daily with a morning view and discussion of our blog. These kids deserved an awesome presentation. I brought all our cook gear, surf gear, and the bike repair kit. I brought the little things as well, such as our assortment of different-sized dry bags for items like maps, cell phone, wallet, and anything else we wanted to keep dry. "Are you ready to go?" I asked Rebecca. When she grumbled her agreement, I playfully countered, "Come on, baby, let's roll," reminding her the school was only a half mile away.

Rebecca did not want to captain the tandem. We had tried a ride together in the early days when I first acquired the bike. Our communication was never very good, and I lacked grace as I shouted from the backseat. She quickly told me I was on my own and she wouldn't ride that thing again. But Rebecca had graciously agreed to help me get the sixteen-foot rig up to the school for the sake of the kids.

We pedaled to the school and pushed the huge visual aid into Madrona's classroom. Rebecca set up the slide show while I broke the bike down. When I started speaking, I heard a boy in the front row whisper to my daughter, "Madrona, that's your dad?" with a sense of awe. His question made me feel like all the time I'd spent on the road, away from home, was worth it.

During the planning stages and our time on the road, people would say, "Wow, that's amazing, that's a long way to pedal." The words might change but their point remained consistent. It was always about the mileage, the number of days on the road, or the athletic endurance it required to carry all the weight it took to be self-sufficient. Some folks were impressed that we had no support vehicle, while others were struck by the creative thinking it took to pack the surfboards and all the other gear. Over the years the praise remained the same, and it's easy to understand why. Initially, the magnitude of the adventure presents itself through the athleticism, self-sufficiency, and ingenuity of our setup. But in truth, the enormity of the achievement lay elsewhere. At least it did for me.

Exercising daily, surfing whenever possible, and sleeping on the road were habits I possessed long before the adventure took shape. I was never concerned about the distance or whether or not I could physically handle the journey. From the beginning I was only concerned about the people: *Could I get enough captains involved? Would everyone want to go? What if the two guys who don't surf get bummed on the trip's focus of looking for waves? What if the schedule doesn't work? Would everyone be OK sleeping under the stars in the dirt? Could I keep everyone stoked? Would everyone have a good time?*

The magnitude of the Bikes, Boards, Blind adventure lay in the challenge of getting so many people together and working toward one goal. The work we did to pedal was the easy stuff. We simply woke up, got on the bike, and in a few hours started looking for a spot to surf. My body got stronger and more used to the routine with each new day. The formula was simply distance divided by time, and we adjusted the ratio depending on how we felt. I could have kept going and pedaled to Chile if anyone had been up for it.

The achievement was in what we did as a group. It was in our time together as friends. It was in the way we hung out like kids. Nobody cared about their phones, their growing or declining number of social media followers, or how many likes they should have on a photo they posted. Our time was spent talking and living in the moment while stuck on a bike together. Most of the time we were laughing, but sometimes we caught up on the serious stuff happening in each other's lives. We had nothing to do all day but pedal, surf, and talk to each other. I felt the simple joy and innocence I had known when I was young, and it was refreshing. Nobody wanted their time on the bike to end, and it's that little fact that I am most proud of. The collaboration alongside great friends to reach a goal, and the way the collaboration pulled many other people together along the way, was the true achievement. And like any major accomplishment, it would be tough to repeat.

On the first day of the adventure, when Temple and I began pedaling away from my house, I wasn't thinking about mileage or conquering any great athletic feat at the finish. I was just excited to hang out with my friend again and go surfing.

Opposite: My brother Blake, me, and Jeff (left to right) on the last day of an awesome adventure. Tijuana border crossing, California. 2013. *Jeff Hawe Collection*

CHAPTER 10

The Medicine of Laughter

I was doing it: flying solo while Rebecca went out. On this evening, nothing would keep me from giving Madrona a five-star meal and a fun time with her new friend. It was going to be a sleepover at our house. Rebecca would be out for the evening in Seattle with her three best friends.

Becca's absence created the perfect opportunity for me to shine—not only as a gourmet cook, but also as the world's best dad. And so I began to create an expectation of awesomeness in my head.

I walked down to our local upscale grocery market. By then I walked everywhere and knew exactly how long it would take me and exactly how much groceries fit into two bags, which was all I wanted to carry home. Going for the good stuff, I was willing to pay extra for words like "regional," "organic," and "sustainable," and for meat that was "grass fed" and "free range."

I did my shopping around the perimeter of the store, following a technique my Aunt Cynthy taught me. "All the healthy food is located around the perimeter of a grocery store," she'd say. "The interior aisles are filled with stuff that will kill you."

Checking out, I pretended to be casual about laying down $200, for which I received the following: a four-pack of Izze soda, four filet mignon steaks, a bag of Yukon gold fingerling potatoes, organic green beans, a fresh loaf of sourdough, stinky cheese, a bottle of wine, two Theo chocolate bars, and some apples. It all fit into two brown bags.

Walking home, I hoped Madrona would remember the dinner later in life while she was attending community college as a result of my "free range" spending habits.

I went to work preparing the meal I knew both Madrona and I love. It had taken me a few years to learn my way around the kitchen again. During the early stages of transition into a new normal, I realized that the kitchen was the most dangerous place for me.

I certainly knew better than to stick my hand in a blender, but I did get stitches in my foot after grabbing a dish towel from the granite countertop. Our largest cutting knife was lying on the towel, and when I pulled on it, the knife fell free and landed on my bare foot.

Rebecca worked with me to create a kitchen system that year. First, we purchased dark blue, pint-sized drinking glasses. The stark color contrast against the light granite counters helped me recognize these glasses; no more knocking over the clear ones I didn't see at all.

We designated specific spots for specific tools and carefully organized things to help me find silverware, utensils, and dishes in the same place every time. For stovetop cooking, it was obvious that electric burners would not work. Gas ranges, when ignited, produce a sound that rises in pitch as the burner output increases. This was one concession to my eyesight that both Becca and I were happy to make, and we picked out a commercial gas range and convection oven.

Soon Madrona and her friend were playing outside and I was setting the table. Everything was coming together just as I saw it in my head.

It was mid-June and our Northwest summer days stay light until 10 p.m., so after finishing my Gorgonzola mash I realized it was already eight o'clock. I set everything out on the table and went to fry the filet mignon on a searing-hot skillet, using a heavy iron sandwich press to weigh the steaks down and cook them fast. This is just how Madrona likes them.

I called the girls inside to sit down and be ready when I served the steaks up hot. Just as I asked, they took a seat, put their napkins on their laps, and I brought out the hot steaks.

Madrona and I got right to it, cutting huge pieces, smiling, and stuffing our mouths, enjoying the steaks in a way we wouldn't if Rebecca were there. Unable to see across the table, I just assumed Madrona's friend was doing the same. But before long, Madrona leaned over and whispered, "She is not happy with her dinner."

Surprised, and in a concerned voice, I asked, "What's the matter, are you not hungry?"

Without hesitation, and with more confidence than many adults would have, she replied, "No, I only eat chicken. But I will also eat pasta if you could make that."

, I was a bit horrified, and as the words left my mouth I heard my grandfather speaking. "You're going to eat that twenty-dollar steak," I said firmly, "that's the only option."

I could sense right off that I was too harsh, even though I couldn't see her face to read her emotions. I couldn't see Madrona's either, but I knew from her response that she was embarrassed by my tone. Graciously, Madrona quickly spoke up: "It's OK, I'll make you some toast with peanut butter."

I apologized to the girls and used all my jokes, but was unable to recover the evening. Before long the girl asked to call her mom, and the night ended without a sleepover. I felt ashamed and angry with myself for not being able to see the social nuances everyone takes for granted.

My personality was becoming more abrupt and slightly rigid, as I often missed social cues. My way of navigating through many social encounters was simply to be blunt and direct. In a world growing more nonconfrontational, I was often misunderstood.

That night, I put Madrona to bed and lay with her for a long time. She'd seen how hard I'd worked to make the meal and knew I was disappointed in how the night turned out. I told her stories of what dinners were like when I was a kid. My mom didn't take requests. One meal was made, and we all finished everything that was served up. I told her I was a grown man before I ever tasted a twenty-dollar steak. When I noticed Madrona had grown quiet, I realized she had fallen asleep.

Later, as I lay in my own bed, I tried to work out why that evening was so hard for me, what my real issue was, and if I could fix it. I was showing up every day to be present in Madrona's life and in many ways, things were getting easier. Still, situations would occur that I never expected, and I would chalk it up to my eyes.

It certainly wasn't about the value of a twenty-dollar steak. At first I blamed the demise of our evening on my not being able to see what was going on at the table. Then I realized my abrupt reaction would have happened even if I'd fully seen things. The fact was that my direct personality made the situation uncomfortable. *Direct is who you are, Devon, and you are not going to be able to change that,* I said to myself.

As I lay overanalyzing the night's events, I recognized that my eyes had nothing to do with our disappointing dinner, and a light bulb went off in my head. I couldn't always worry about my eyes—they weren't always going to be the problem. I realized that even with perfect vision, that evening would have gone south: I would have been just as direct, and Madrona's friend would have been just as sensitive. It was in this moment that I started to feel OK.

Since so much in my world had changed, I wondered if the basic things I wanted from life remained the same. *What is it you want out of life in this moment?* I asked myself.

I want to play outdoors. I want to work hard. I want Rebecca to have an exciting life. I want to shine in my daughter's eyes. I want to make my friends and family laugh, and I want to laugh with them. *That's pretty much it,* I thought. *Not much has changed at all.* And then I went to sleep.

Our house had become one of the primary spots where Madrona hung out with her friends. A trampoline helped in this regard, but I also like to think she felt comfortable bringing everybody here as well. Since her friends were always at the house, they became a part of my new summer focus along with Madrona.

In the spirit of my recent epiphany, I spent the rest of the summer coming up with fresh ways to keep Madrona and her friends playing outdoors and off their screens. Since laughter might be even more important than playing outside, I felt obligated to teach Madrona and her friends all the pranks I knew of.

As a way of including the value of hard work into our summer goal of constantly being outside, Madrona and I created a small community service group we called GLAM GALS. The acronym

The GLAM GALS on their way to pick up neighborhood trash. Bainbridge Island, Washington. 2014. *Rebecca Raney*

stands for Girls Living A More Giving, Adventuresome Lifestyle. Our mission was basic. The goal of GLAM GALS was to pick up trash in the community we lived in. About a dozen girls, another parent, Madrona, and I met once a week at our house and walked the mile and a half to downtown Bainbridge, picking up trash along the way. Then we chose a different street to walk home on and picked up trash on that road as well. Madrona and I visited the Bainbridge Island Parks and Rec coordinator and asked her if the city would provide the gloves, reflective vests, and bags needed. She was stoked and not only agreed to supply the safety stuff, but also told Madrona that the mayor would issue a certificate for each girl that validated the number of community service hours she had accrued at the end of the summer.

When school started in the fall, every participant had an impressive fifty hours of community service. Personally, it was the best and most basic charity I had ever seen. There was no drama; who could say anything negative about picking up trash?

As a parent, I noticed three positive things that I would not have predicted. First was the way our walking routine taught the girls the topography of the land around them. On many occasions I would hear someone in the group say, "I didn't realize this was such a big hill, even though I go up and down it all the time in a car." I had taken for granted the fact that I understood the landscape around me as a kid because I was rarely in a car and rode my bike everywhere.

The girls also officially learned our zip code after we made T-shirts, and they wanted a way to identify the group as being from Bainbridge Island. Not a single GLAM GAL knew our zip code until we put the digits on the back of our T-shirt. It made me wonder if they had ever sent a postcard or mailed a letter.

Toward the middle of the summer came the most pleasant surprise. I noticed the group never bickered, tried to outdo each other, or even complained as we fell into the consistent routine of picking up trash. It was obvious to me that our success came from keeping our mission basic and focused on one goal.

Our local newspaper ran an article on the GLAM GALS that summer, and my favorite quote is from Madelyn Harris: "We're the next generation. It's better than just sitting. We're doing something."

A little more fun than the community service were the pranks, and I spent an equal number of hours teaching the girls, at their request, a myriad of practical jokes. These pranks were always designed to be witty and clever, but never to hurt a person's feelings. It wasn't long before they were coming up with a few new pranks of their own.

The result was nonstop giggles, screams, and laughs. On one of our first official pranking outings I walked with Madrona and her friends downtown, where we super-glued eight quarters on top of a concrete bench located in front of a coffee shop. Then we all sat across the street and watched random pedestrians try really, really hard to pick up the quarters. Frustrated, most people left after a few tries, but some folks came back just a few minutes later with a strengthened resolve.

Next came the dollar bill prank. I taped fishing line to the back of a dollar bill, and the girls laid it on the ground at the grocery store or coffee shop and tried to get someone to reach for it. Most folks knew of this trick already; they would laugh and then tell the girls they were cute. Without fail, during the few times we tried to make this prank work, one of the girls would ask, "Can we use a twenty?" I would laugh and say, "Sure! Do you have a twenty?"

We moved on to the purse prank. I tied fishing line to the handle of an old, but not ugly, purse that Rebecca said we could use. Then we laid the handbag at the edge of our driveway just off the sidewalk. The girls rolled out as much line as needed and then hid around the corner of the house, but still within sight of the purse. They waited for a jogger or walker to pass by and eye their shiny bait. If the person reached for the bag, one of the girls would yank the line and a chorus of laughter would erupt.

Some of my pranks were outdated or uncool, and the girls quickly designed their own variation to bring them up to date. "Devon, do you have any jokes for us today?" they once asked. I suggested that they call their grandparents, so we weren't dialing random strangers, and ask if the fridge is running, and then tell Grandpa or Grandma to go and catch it before it runs away. Madrona politely informed me that this one was lame and they already had their own prank calls. Later in the summer, I overheard Madrona and Hannah Burt calling McDonald's to make a dinner reservation for two.

Sometimes I had to draw the line and be an un-fun parent. "We are going to ding-dong-ditch," they said, referring to the prank where a person walks up and rings the doorbell at a random house and then simply runs off. "No," I promptly replied, "that one is super annoying. Plus, you guys need to be more creative than that. It's not even a funny prank."

One of the girls had a teenage sister, and with their mom's permission, we put the sister's car on Craigslist. The girls took a screenshot of the same model, but brand-new, off the Dodge website and then wrote, "Leaving country, must sell, runs great, perfect condition, low mileage, awesome stereo, $700," followed by, "I work the graveyard shift, please call before 5 a.m." By nine the following morning she had answered the phone twenty times. Confused at first, she wondered why her parents were selling the Dodge Neon. Soon she figured out the joke, became annoyed, stopped answering the phone, and by noon she had let forty more calls go to voice-mail. Then we cancelled the listing. I enjoyed watching the girls write the clever description, but part of me wondered if I had gone too far with this one.

The season's most popular prank, and the one that provided the widest variety of application, always involved a toilet and a Hershey's chocolate bar. Slightly warmed up in the microwave and then smeared on a toilet seat, a piece of malleable Hershey can prompt a host of reactions.

So I was not too surprised when Madrona and her friend played a variation of this prank on us adults one Friday night.

I built a fire in our outdoor pit, Rebecca poured some wine, and we invited over Madrona's new friend's mother. We had not met her yet and since our girls were hanging out a bunch, we were looking forward to getting to know her.

She was great, and hanging around the fire together was easy. The girls began to act out skits and practice their jokes, while our job was to be the audience. The impromptu drama routines were played out on our deck, elevated a few feet off the ground. To us, sitting lower on the concrete patio, it was like watching a stage performance.

Soon the girls were out of jokes, and whispering in my ear, Madrona solicited suggestions from her dad, the shenanigans expert. Playing it cool, I announced to everyone that I was going inside to help the girls find the marshmallows for S'mores. Once in the kitchen, I called for a huddle and we all agreed to prank the new mom with our recently developed shocker we called "the soiled briefs."

The dirty underwear prank is basic, just like it sounds, and had been perfected by Madrona and her friends that summer. After purchasing a pack of new men's white briefs, she would go to work making them look worn, stained, and grubby. She achieved the look by soaking the new underwear in green tea, rubbing them vigorously in the grass, and then playing tug-of-war with the elastic band. The look was completed by smearing the inseam with chocolate sauce and melted Hershey.

It never got old. They'd leave the "soiled" whities in the front yard, then pick them up with mock horror as a neighbor walked by. With rehearsed drama, the girls would freak out with so much overacting that after a second or two the neighbor would always realize it was a joke. The performance had undeniable shock value.

Madrona's friend would play the lead role and bring out the undergarment after supposedly finding it in our powder room. The prank went down like this:

I returned to my seat by the fire, passed around the marshmallows, and resumed normal conversation. Minutes later, the girls came outside to join us and informed us the skits were done for the night. After sitting for a short bit, Madrona's friend stood up and asked politely, "Mr. Raney, where is your bathroom?" I responded with directions to the downstairs one and then she said to her mom, "I'll be right back."

A few minutes went by, enough for us all to forget she was gone, and then the friend returned to the deck. She stood with her arm outstretched, dangling the stained underwear from one finger, as if trying to keep them as far away from her body as possible.

"Mr. Raney," the friend announced, "I found these on the floor by the toilet."

With fictitious concern, I jumped up from my chair, and on cue Madrona screamed, "Oh my God!"

At which point Madrona's friend hit her mark by saying, "Maybe it's just chocolate." And then for effect slowly sniffed them.

Rebecca, both girls, and I burst into hysterics. Seeing our reactions, the friend's mom realized it had to be a prank. She let out a sigh, and said, "Oh my God, that's disgusting even if it is chocolate," and then began to laugh as well.

Silently, around the fire, I let the laughter fall on me like a blanket. The sound was pure joy, and it echoed in my head like a melody. There was no social awkwardness caused by my eyes in those moments, and I felt the laughter work like medicine.

In many circles my Parental Pranking Plan is probably frowned upon. At first glance I might even agree. My approach, however, has never been flippant. It was a summer spent intentionally teaching my daughter what was good to find funny. Kids are taught, in one way or another, everything they learn. When it came to laughter, I wanted to be my kid's teacher. Laughter can

Opposite: If they are laughing we must be doing something right. Mount Baker, Washington. New Year's Eve, 2017. *Rebecca Raney*

heal, bond, break the ice, break down barriers, restore, keep us living longer, and strengthen a bruised heart.

My focus was always on teaching Madrona how to laugh at the prank and never the person. To come up with a trick and then see if it works takes a creative process, but to target a person is a malicious thing. I wanted to teach Madrona the difference. Seeing a random person reach for a dollar bill is funny because it took some thinking and effort to get that person to go for it. But it has nothing to do with the individual person.

It wasn't just the girls who were being taught how to laugh. I was learning again as well. Gradually, since my eye diagnosis, my sarcastic nature became a little more pointed and with a bitter tinge. I've always had a sharp wit, but I had begun to use it more harshly and a little less humorously. As things became healthier in my soul I was able to spot the cobwebs around my laughing muscles. Madrona, her friends, and our summer of pranks brushed the webs away and set me laughing in the right direction again.

CHAPTER 11

Work Ethic and Heart

The Boeing 737 revved up its engines, the pilot released the brakes, and we began bouncing down the runway. Rebecca reached over and grabbed my hand, held it tight, and lay her head on my shoulder.

"Are you excited?" I asked.

"Yes. I need this. I'm tired," she said. It was October 8, 2015, two years after the Boards, Bikes, Blind trip.

"I hope this month helps you relax," I replied. "The house is on the beach. I won't need a ride to go surfing, so you can do whatever you want in the sun all day." I assured her that after a month in Baja, we would come home recharged and ready for the work we needed to do at the coffee shop. The construction portion of the remodel and rebrand of our business would hit when we got home and was scheduled to complete in the spring.

Four hours later we landed in Cabo San Lucas, Baja California. In my early teens I had been to Baja plenty of times, or at least I had crossed the border into Tijuana plenty of times. Usually I intended to reach Ensenada, seventy miles deep, which in my mind was the heart of Baja. Occasionally I made it all the way to Rosarito, sixteen miles south. But more often than not I got hung up in Tijuana. I was young, not yet driving, and hanging out with a loose crowd. In reality, those trips were a nightmare, and never about surf or adventure. They were sketchy, and to this day I don't like to think about those times.

When we picked up our rental car, things were not as Rebecca had anticipated. The rental terms were different from those she had discussed over the phone, and despite adding Mexico service to Becca's Verizon plan, her iPhone didn't pull up the maps or dial any numbers. I stood helplessly as her expectation of a relaxing vacation started to fade away. I desperately hoped I could help get things back on track.

It was dark out. We spent too much time at the car rental, we paid double for the vehicle, and soon we would be driving into El Pescadero in the dark. I knew we needed to find the highway and then we would be good. The job fell on Becca to use her eyes to watch for signs. What I believed would be easy had become stressful as Becca firmly stated, "There are no street signs." Southern Baja had been hit hard during the hurricane season that year and most of the signs were down. Soon we were lost and driving around a rural barrio. Becca didn't like driving in our current situation, and I felt a painful twang as I told her, "I really wish that I could drive." Stopping at a gas station, I spoke in my broken Mexican street slang and asked for a map. Unable to see it, I turned it over to Becca, feeling like I was handing her just one more burden.

Since my flip phone was able to make calls, I tried to help by calling the local guy who had the keys to the house. I told him we would be at the only gas station in El Pescadero in an hour. When we showed up, he was waiting on his quad, drinking a Corona. We followed him down a four-mile, rutted dirt road until we could hear the surf. When we reached the house we'd rented—isolated, rural, and built on a low spot just a stone's throw from the water—my first impression was, "This is paradise."

After I moved our bags inside, I sat with Becca and Madrona on the rooftop patio until we could no longer keep our sleepy eyes open. The two of them described the waves, visible by moonlight, and I knew they were peeling perfectly by the way they were exploding on the beach. Elated, the three of us went to bed, choosing to sleep in the same room that first night. Becca and I took the

Opposite: Rebecca beach fishing in the early-morning shorepound in Baja, Mexico. 2018.
Colin Wiseman

big bed, and Madrona laid cushions down on the floor at the foot of it. She went to sleep listening to a book on her iPod.

In the morning, Becca went downstairs to start the coffee. Initially I heard her speaking, but I couldn't make out what she was saying. Then she began yelling, "My laptop is missing and backpack is missing!" Then I heard her scream, "The safe is open, our cash is gone. Our passports are gone—it's empty!" Sprinting back up to our bedroom, she said, "Oh my God, they stole my iPhone off the nightstand; I left it right there," as she pointed to the small dresser located just inches from where she laid her head. She looked over at Madrona asleep on the floor, I heard a sickening gasp, and then, "They took her iPod from under her arm." My eyes closed as the words hit me, as if my eyelids might protect me from what the words meant.

Our surfboards, fishing poles, and what clothing we had put in drawers were all that remained. While Becca stayed in the room with Madrona, I went downstairs to try to get a sense of what had happened. Mostly I just thought about how we were going to get more cash, since our bank cards were gone. The safe had been locked, but they had found the key in Becca's nightstand drawer. I couldn't believe the intruders had opened that drawer and I never woke up.

The house was the cheapest monthly rental we could find within walking distance to a surf spot. It was remote, with solar power and water tanks on the rooftop, and no landline. As I took a seat next to Rebecca on the front patio, I noticed the home was built in a low spot and visible to everything around us. "I found our passports in the dirt over there," she said, pointing. Staring out at the ocean, as if in a trance, Becca said, "They were in our room, walking around, and we didn't wake up. It's like the scariest part of a movie." I thought about how true her analogy was.

Reluctantly, Becca said, "I think we should go home."

Frustrated, I spoke too firmly. "We are staying. What will Madrona learn if we pack it up on day one?" It seemed to me that going home was the quick and easy fix. The tougher choice was to stay and figure it out. Throughout my life, not just since my eye diagnosis, this approach has benefited me in some way, and I simply believed staying was the right decision for all of us in that moment. I had tunnel vision. I saw our situation as an obstacle to overcome. "You have to go to know," which had served me so well, had now started to morph into "You have to stay to know." I truly believed something good would come from it, but I forgot all about the real reason we were there in the first place: It was going to be a relaxing and restorative month for Rebecca.

"We don't even have the money to get out of here anyway," Becca said with resignation.

Since my flip phone was in a small bag with my toothbrush, it had not been found by the thieves. I doubt they would have taken it anyway. I powered up my phone and tried to make a call while Rebecca continued to sit, silent and motionless. "Now we can add cell service to our growing list of things that are not available at this house," I said with frustration. Rebecca did not respond. "We need to drive to Cabo so we can start making calls," I continued. When we walked around back to get in the car, all four of the vehicle doors were open wide. "I guess they found the car keys on the counter," I said. Then we added sunglasses, maps, my backpack, and a hat to the list of stolen items.

In the city we found a café and spent a few hours making calls to the States. First to my parents, then Rebecca's, then the bank, then our coffee shop, and on and on until we stopped to conserve the phone's battery.

Later in the day, Cressa Campos was arriving from Oregon. Becca had been looking forward to a week of fun on the beach with her lifelong friend. Cressa's husband, Lars, and their three kids were also coming, and I did not look forward to telling them about the robbery. We waited at the café in Cabo so that I could receive their call. After they landed, rented their car, and got in touch, we met up at a taco stand on Highway 19. They followed us back to the house, and I desperately hoped our second night would be the fresh start we needed.

But it wasn't. After I told Lars and Cressa about the previous night's robbery, they were just as on edge as we were. They chose not to tell their kids, so the three Campos siblings were the only ones to fall asleep. Madrona was skittish, and would jump up and look out the window every time she heard a sound.

Becca saw the truck long before it reached our house. "Somebody is coming," she said. It was 2 a.m. when they showed up and started shining their spotlight through our windows. The vehicle had local police markings, busted-out taillights, and flashers on the roof that were not illuminated. Two guys got out, wearing uniforms, and started shouting "¡Salgan afuera!" (Come outside!) "Todo está bien, solo queremos hablar." (Everything's okay, we just want to talk.) I had flashbacks to the Tijuana days of my youth. I had been told to keep a twenty-dollar bill in my sock, "for emergencies." On two occasions I gave my twenty to an officer so that he would leave me alone. In truth, I don't even know if he wanted it; I couldn't understand him, so I just handed it over and went on my way.

Two in the morning didn't seem like the time to chat—we didn't have any cash anyway—so the door stayed closed. Inside, behind the front door, I held a kitchen knife and Lars gripped an aluminum baseball bat he had found in the closet. Later, Lars took a closer look at the bat and noticed it had a bunch of significant dents, like it had been beating on something very hard. I wondered why a person would need that bat, and why it was so easy to find.

No one in our group said a word, and eventually the two men in the truck left. Then we all took a post at a different window. Still gripping the kitchen knife, I mentally rehearsed the different scenarios that could have played out the night before had I woken up during the robbery.

I had been in many fights when I was a kid and even a few as a young adult. There was never one person who was solely to blame and never a clear winner. In fact, there was no winner at all, only two losers. A fistfight is an ugly thing, but I am grateful to have come away from those times with a basic understanding of physical violence. At my core, regardless of how I had grown to see fighting as an extension of hate, I remained unafraid of the physical aspect. I did not subscribe to the idea that practicing a formal fighting technique would help me protect my family. I simply knew, from time spent in unfortunate situations, that if an altercation were ever to occur in the presence of my wife or daughter, I could handle whatever beating came with the action I took to get them out of that moment.

As the hours ticked away, and night gave way to morning, I questioned whether or not I should still be so confident. Would I have been able to hear where the intruders stood in the room and go after them by sound? Or would I have to ask Becca where the intruders were and then move quickly? How would I know if they had a weapon? At the very least, I could keep Madrona and Rebecca behind me and physically put my body between them and whoever came at us. I started to get angry at my eyes again, as I had so many times before, as I recognized how my blindness would be a much bigger roadblock in that situation than I'd imagined. Bitterness began to seep in with the anger. I was tired of being in new situations where my eyes presented new ways to help me fail. I thought I was past all that.

I was hung up on my own perception of protection. Rebecca would tell me much later that she didn't care at all about being protected physically during that trip, but that I had failed to protect her emotionally. She would also tell me that for the first time in our marriage, she had been afraid to say how she truly felt because my resolve to power on had become so absolute. I didn't know any of this at the time.

In the morning I went outside with Lars. "Your rental has a flat," he said grimly. The car tire had a screw with only half of its length pushed into the tread; had we picked it up on the road, it would have been set flush with the rubber.

Lars and I changed the tire, packed the car, and then it began to rain hard. Within an hour the dirt road was a snotty red mess, and our cars could not climb the hill that led from the beach up to the highway. We went back inside the house for a new plan. Soon both our families were walking south on the beach and over a headland that separated us from a different beach. We found a small tourist-oriented resort a few miles away. I had to borrow the money from Lars to pay for the expensive beachfront hotel. We said how we hoped our ladies would relax. In truth, we hoped the two of us would relax as well.

The rain stopped on our second day at the resort. Soon the dirt roads were dry and hard from the hot sun, and both Lars and Rebecca walked back to the robbery house to retrieve the rental cars. Every day Rebecca and I had to negotiate with the owner of the house, who lived in San Diego. I lobbied heavily for a full refund, but the process was slow since we were communicating through VRBO. Once it was clear to the owner what had happened, she refunded our deposit and the full month's rent without delay. After that was finally resolved, there were only two days left before Cressa would be leaving, and Rebecca had not enjoyed a relaxing—let alone reenergizing—moment with her close friend. Cressa and her family left for Oregon. If I had been able to recognize how truly necessary it was for Becca to recharge her batteries, then that would have been the logical time for us to go back home too, to cut our losses and regroup in familiar surroundings. Instead, I pushed forward. It was the only way I knew, and I still believed that something good would come out of the traumatic experience that was now almost two weeks behind us.

Rebecca said she was tired and didn't want to make any decisions. However, she agreed to look for a house, and she found one located just ten miles to the north in Todos Santos. It was small and secure, with a concrete wall around the perimeter, and the owners lived nearby in town. She paid for seventeen days, the remainder of our trip.

I had heard a quality wave existed in Todos Santos, but I wasn't going to ask other surfers how to get there. On principle, as a surfer, I would have to find it on my own—or more accurately, with the help of Rebecca. Our new rental house was just a mile from the beach, and soon the three of us were taking long walks along the shoreline in both directions. With Becca's description of the waves, the shore, and where the surfers were located, it wasn't long before I believed I'd found the spot. Then I showed up there every morning at sunup for the next sixteen days. If the wind backed down, I paddled out there at sunsets, too.

It was Rebecca, again, who made my early-morning missions possible. She woke up before dawn, drove us down the dirt road, and then took photos of the sunrise or rested on her blanket. Madrona, despite the robbery trauma, was able to stay sleeping until we returned later in the morning. I considered this a positive thing, a win if you will, but I failed to support Rebecca in her need to rest.

On the second or third morning, a surfer said hello to me on the beach and I fell into a pleasant conversation. Polite, respectful, complimentary, and not in a hurry, the man seemed to belong to the generation older than mine, but I couldn't get a sense of how old he really was. Later I learned he had just turned fifty. His name was Ricardo, and while we were talking I learned that we had met earlier in the week at the busy surfing beach Cerritos. I apologized to Ricardo for not recognizing him or realizing we had met, and then I told him about my eyesight. "You surf good for having bad eyes," he laughed.

Finally, I connected the dots when I got a close-up look at his lengthy board and powerful, stocky frame. This was the guy Lars warned me about, the one who was catching all those long rights out at the rock and then freight-training down the line. "He is going fast and not stopping for anyone," Lars had said. I told this to Ricardo, who laughed, liking the compliment. He said, "I am going fast because down-the-line is my main move these days."

The next morning I showed up at sunrise, paddled out, and tried to keep a respectful distance from others already in the water. I assumed Ricardo was one of them, and my assumption was proved correct when he paddled over to me and said, "Come with me—the best takeoff is over here." I went, and soon he was introducing me to a few of the regulars. I met Coach and a few others who had a grip on the morning session. Most of them were Ricardo's age, and they all had a relaxed, patient approach. I felt right at home. On the beach, I mentioned to Ricardo that I didn't drive because of my eyes and that it would be rad for Rebecca to sleep in. Without hesitation he offered to pick me up the next morning, and this became the routine for most of the trip. I considered it another win for the family.

One morning as we drove away from the beach, Ricardo said, "You really don't see much, do you?" For many people, this realization often came much later in the relationship, so I was very familiar with the question and what he would likely say next.

"No, I don't see much. It's hard to describe and an even harder thing to understand. How can you tell?" I asked.

"This morning you got a nice one and then you paddled back and sat right next to me. I was about to say, 'Nice wave' when you shouted, 'Ricardo?' looking for me," he said as he started laughing. "I thought, *Damn, I am right in front of this guy and he doesn't know it's me.*" I laughed with him at the absurdity of how it must seem, and then he asked me the question I had heard so many times since my diagnosis. "How are you able to still surf?" he asked.

Next spread: Going left, pig-dog style, and hoping for the tube. Baja, Mexico. 2017.
Colin Wiseman

I tried to explain the best I could how things work for me out there. "Contrast is a huge deal," I started. "These morning sessions are the best for me because the sun is lighting up the wave faces and there is no brightness behind them. The wave faces turn dark blue against the soft blue background of the sky and slightly silver ocean behind the wave, creating contrast all around. Sunset is much harder, when everything is bright behind the wave and there is no contrast between the shady, flat ocean disappearing into the horizon and the actual wave face heading toward me."

"I can see that," Ricardo said.

"I have also had to change the way I surf. I don't really paddle to get into waves anymore," I said. "Instead I drop late, like a skateboarder on a ramp. I spin around after the wave stands up and slip my board under my feet at the last minute."

"I see you do that all the time. You are like a little jackrabbit out there, popping out of the lip at the last minute and then pig-dogging," he said, referring to the term used when surfers go backside, grab rail, and sit low as they make their bottom turn. Ricardo burst into hysterics as he teased my pig-dog style.

"It also helps when the waves have some good juice, and it helps me if they consistently break at the same spot. That's why I like these waves here so much," I said. "They stand up at the same spot on the rock reef every time, and they are punchy. Once I am in the wave, the sides of my eyes can pick up contrast and movement. When a wave is peeling, or has enough shape to provide a curling pocket, I can still surf. The contrast between the whitewater created by the breaking part of the wave and the smooth blue wall ahead of that breaking section is recognizable to my eyes. The definition between the two colors is strongest at the point where the wave is just starting to break over itself. I try to stay as deep in the pocket as possible.

"When I am in the water my eyes cannot see super-small waves," I continued. "Without some size, they look like speed bumps and are not noticeable to me until they are already passing by. However, if the swell has some size, organization, and nice spacing, my eyes catch the movement and the shapes appear against the horizon looking like garden hedges."

I told Ricardo that if the winds are side shore or onshore, I am unable to surf at all. The chop created by the cross pattern, or the crumbling effect created by wind blowing from behind the wave, all looks like other waves to me. In these conditions I get confused, and have many times wasted energy paddling for feathery wind ripples.

"I would always rather surf with a friend, a guy like you, Ricardo, who is comfortable shouting out verbal cues than go out alone."

It had felt like a long explanation, and I paused for a moment while I searched for a way to articulate the most important thing to me. "Sometimes, Ricardo, I will catch a wave and surf it perfectly. Paddling back to the peak, past surfers who don't know me and who are unaware of my vision impairment, I will sometimes hear the congratulatory 'Nice wave,' and I know it has nothing to do with my disability. It is in these moments that I feel completely capable on a level nothing else provides. Who knows, Ricardo, maybe the only reason I am still sideways is because being in the water is the one place where I feel least blind."

After every surf session I returned happy and energetic, and I tried to convince myself that by doing so, Rebecca's spirits would lift alongside mine. But I was wrong, and she continued retreating into herself. However, we worked hard together to ensure Madrona found positive experiences in Mexico. We took her to a turtle release, where she was able to watch the pancake-sized babies break through their shells and scratch toward the shorepound. On our last full day in Todos, we visited the local orphanage. Becca put together an art project, and Madrona saw how happy the kids were in spite of having literally nothing. I was simply proud to be Becca's husband as I again saw her exude quiet confidence through the effort she put into teaching a painting lesson to the young orphans. As we flew back to Washington the next day, I hoped we had at least departed on a good note.

After we returned home to Bainbridge Island, Rebecca started mentioning how she felt tired, even exhausted, all day long. "I could just keep sleeping," she said while we drank our coffee in bed one morning. She would also tell me that I needed to slow down. I took these statements as jabs at the way I had failed to give her the time she needed to recharge in Mexico. But underhanded comments and passive-aggressive remarks are not Becca's way. She was simply telling me how she felt.

It was already mid-November, and soon we would be moving our snow gear into our Mount Baker cabin. I reminded myself again and again that once at Baker as a family, snowboarding together, the three of us would feel refreshed and united. I held my hope in winter.

During this time, I received an e-mail from Josh Dirksen asking if I was headed for Bend, Oregon, that December for the annual Dirksen Derby. Embarrassed that I had missed the entry date cutoff, I quickly responded that of course we wouldn't miss the Derby, and I explained that we had been away in Mexico.

The Dirksen Derby is a banked slalom race, founded by Josh in partnership with his sponsor Patagonia. Strictly a charity event, all proceeds go to Tyler Eklund, a talented snowboarder who became paralyzed in an accident while training for the 2007 USA Snowboard Association National Championships. The Derby was born out of a need to help a friend.

The Derby has become a special event for the three of us. My family feels connected, each in our own way, and I feel the obvious need to show up and support Tyler.

Rebecca has done artwork for the annual Broken Board Art Auction. This event, held on the eve of the finals, auctions off donated artwork from talented artists in and around the snowboard community. She carved a landscape of waves, trees, and snowcapped mountains into the fiberglass on one of my old surfboards, then gave it definition and color by pushing inks into the cuts, then wiping the top clean. Carving with small hand tools, Rebecca worked more than sixty hours on the project. I thought it was awesome and selfishly wished we had kept it.

Madrona has competed in the race every year since 2012 and looks forward to the Derby because it's her first event of the year, our family's first snowboard trip, and is close to Christmas. She likes to go out to dinner in downtown Bend and look at all the lights.

In my e-mail exchange with Josh, I sent a few surf photos from our time down south. I briefly mentioned our trip but didn't tell him the details. Stoked on the photos, Josh asked if he could use

Opposite: Madrona tuning into her competitive side before she drops into what will become her first-place run at the 2017 Dirksen Derby. Mount Bachelor, Oregon. *Tim Stanford*

one of them. I wasn't totally sure what he meant, but I trusted Josh completely and would do anything for the Derby. I said of course he could and didn't give it another thought.

A few weeks later, in the evening, after saying good night to Madrona, Rebecca came into our room and said, "I need to read you something." She sounded serious, or slightly choked up, but I couldn't tell for sure.

Giving her my full attention, I said, "Okay, did something happen?"

"No," she said. "Josh posted a wave shot of you on Instagram and said some very kind things." The way she spoke gave me goose bumps, and I could tell she had read the post a few times already.

The photo was of me surfing backside in Todos Santos. Rebecca took the shot while sitting on the beach with Madrona. What Josh said was this:

"November 19, 2015. I just saw this photo of Devon Raney surfing down in Mexico recently, and it made me appreciate the incredible crew of people who make it out to the Derby every year. Devon is a blind snowboarder who rips at all things sideways. If I had to make a list of the most impressive athletes I have ever met, Devon would be one of the top guys."

When she finished reading, we both felt an overwhelming sense of gratitude. The kindness was a huge surprise. I started getting the familiar feeling of uneasiness I get anytime someone gives me a big compliment. Normally, I try to deflect or downplay the person's words, but in this case they were out there and even if I felt undeserving, I couldn't do a thing about it.

"Those are some big words coming from Josh," I said in awe. "It's ironic really. The last time I cared about being an impressive athlete was in high school."

As a kid, I had wanted to be a gifted athlete for as far back as I can remember. My dad, who played a few years of junior college basketball, kept up on sports. I knew who his favorite basketball players were because he referred to them as "gifted athletes." Also, every team I was on had a standout player, and we all referred to that person as "the gifted athlete."

My uncle Larry was the head basketball coach for thirty-five years at Santa Barbara High School. He was gruff, direct, a little macho, and always laughing. He was super fun to be around, and larger than life in my eyes. Married to my dad's oldest sister, Larry was not only my dad's hero, but also the older brother my dad never had.

Anytime I hooked up with Uncle Larry, he would skip any formal hello and jump right into the solid life advice he had for me. He'd say stuff like, "I heard there is a drug epidemic among hippie surfers. Don't go doing that stuff, Dev." Then, like a born coach, he would remind me of the hard work required to become a great athlete, followed by his list of the gifted ones. Larry named his dog Magic, after the all-time greatest, Magic Johnson. So I grew up believing a gifted athlete was very tall, strong, probably black, and super excited about basketball.

During the summer, when sixth-grade select soccer teams were just beginning to be a thing, a regional team was being formed and I showed up for the tryouts.

The workouts went for two days. Three regulation soccer fields were marked out with a different coach at each field. Rotating through each station, we performed exercises and drills so the coaches could get a feel for our skill level. My dad remembers the weekend well, and he conservatively estimates that 250 kids were trying out for the new team.

The head coach called our house one evening the following week. My parents came into my room and my dad proudly gave me the news. "You made the team," he said. "They took fifteen, and you were the fifteenth pick. Your coach said you displayed heart and a hard work ethic." Both my mom and dad were beaming with pride. I was flat-out horrified.

I did not want to be picked last, be known for having heart, or be viewed as the team workhorse. I wanted a phone call saying I was a gifted athlete and that they couldn't build the team without me. The fact that I was chosen over 235 other kids was completely lost on me. None of those kids received a phone call, but I was too hung up on the word "gifted" to recognize my achievement.

I worked hard that season. Playing my role of team motivator, I never missed a practice and always did what the coach said. It was a winning season and we took the championship. I vividly remember the trophy, because it was taller than me and I was only allowed to keep it at my house for a short time before it went to a different player's house. The following year we didn't do as well, and the trophy moved on to another town.

I get embarrassed when I look back and realize how hung up I was on the words "gifted athlete."

Rebecca enlarged the photo on our desktop computer and I did my best to stare at it. I put my face up to the screen as I tried to see more. Looking at myself in the pocket of the wave, I realized it must be very hard for a person who does not know me to comprehend the extent of my vision loss.

When Rebecca reentered the room and saw that I hadn't moved, she asked, "What are you thinking about?"

"Do you think people generally get how bad my eyes are?" And before she could answer, I blurted, "I don't think anyone has a clue!"

Rebecca laughed at this and said, "You already know what I think."

She was right, I did already know, but she has a strong opinion on the matter, so I prodded, "No, I forget—tell me again."

"Of course nobody has a clue how much you can't see." She went on, "It's your own fault for pretending everything is fine all the time." I was aware that her statement was really about her more than it was about me.

"That fact is harder for you, isn't it?" I asked.

"Well, yes, you know it is. I watch you act as if things are fine, and pretend you don't need help, but I know you well." Thinking about her words, she paused for a second. "I know you wish your friends would pick you up to go surfing, and I know you wish they would offer to snowboard with you. But I also understand why you don't ask for help. There are times you shouldn't have to."

She paused again and then finished softly, "Because you don't share with people about your eyes, I end up being the only person who gets it. This can be a lonely place."

"Bringing attention to my disability is a slippery slope, a perilous balancing act, and a double-edged sword," I said. We both laughed at how easily the truth can be found in clichés.

I enjoyed her laughter. "Do you remember when I was the first-ever blind waterslide monitor at the YMCA?" I asked sarcastically.

Laughing some more, Rebecca said, "Yes, that was awesome." And she knew where I was headed. I continued with growing enthusiasm as I recounted the story:

Opposite: The Instagram shot that inspired Josh Dirksen to speak so kindly of me. Baja, Mexico. 2015. *Rebecca Raney*

During that first year of our family's major adjustment, I was taking Madrona to the YMCA every day. I was learning to use the Gig Harbor city bus as well.

Every time the two of us went swimming, without fail Madrona wanted to ride down the waterslide. It was mind-boggling, but every day the damn thing was closed. So finally I asked one of the lifeguards when it would actually be open. He said, "Never midday. We only have enough staff to man the slide during peak operating hours." Then the lifeguard finished by saying, "If you want, I can teach you how to become a volunteer slide monitor, and then you can open the slide for everyone anytime you like."

I just stood there blankly for a second before it hit me: He doesn't have a clue about my eyes.

When I realized my opportunity, I naturally agreed to be a slide monitor. Excited, the lifeguard began the process by taking Madrona and me over to the slide and showing us the gate valve beneath the stair ladder, which opened up the water flow for the giant toy. I couldn't see it, but I nodded and kept agreeing with everything he said. I was confident Madrona saw the valve and knew she could help me open it at a later time. Next, the guard took me up to the top and we let a few kids slide down. He kept instructing me on how much space I should give before I let the next kid drop. Pointing down at the pool, he would say, "Don't let the next kid go until the previous one has swum over to those steps." Smiling, I just kept nodding as I tried to stare in the direction in which he was pointing. In my head, I was figuring I would just give the kids seven seconds after I heard the splash of them hitting the water before I sent the next one down.

Finally, the lesson came to an end and the guard told me I would need to sign a liability release. "No problem," I said confidently. He went to get the paper and while he was gone, I asked Madrona to show me where the signature line was when he returned. The lifeguard brought back a pen with him, handed me a form, and I held it vertically against the wall. Madrona helped line my hand up with the signature line and I signed the thing without being able to see any of it. He didn't have a clue how bad my vision was.

Stoked, I proudly handed the form back to the lifeguard, and I was able to run the waterslide all summer long for Madrona and her friends.

Rebecca and I were in hysterics as I finished retelling the story. We continued laughing as we thought about all those kids I sent down the slide and how the YMCA officially cleared a blind guy for the job.

Smiling, we sat in silence for a little bit longer. Rebecca was the first to get up, and on her way out the door she turned and said, "I get it—it's more rewarding to figure things out and feel normal."

Josh's words had a powerful impact on me because they forced me to take a deep look at how and why I am able to still perform as an athlete. Since the moment my eyes began to fail me, I have been trying to prove to myself that I can still show up for my passions. I have been trying to prove to myself that I can still surf, and that I can still snowboard.

I like to think Josh Dirksen's Instagram post was simply a nod to the effort I have put into chasing my passions with a vision impairment. I believe he knows many athletes much more impressive than myself, but his compliment felt good regardless. For as great as it felt to be called an impressive athlete, I'm really just thankful for the work ethic and heart that I have. I doubt my dad cared too much if I made the soccer team or not. Dad was proud to hear I showed heart and a strong work ethic, knowing those two gifts would take me further in life than anything else. But I would often think of Josh's words during a moment when I needed a boost or a smile.

Soon I was loading our truck, and the three of us started out driving to Bend for the Derby. Somewhere near the border between Washington and Oregon, Rebecca said, "I have been getting this weird tingling in my hands and feet. It's mostly when I drive. It feels like electricity."

CHAPTER 12

Slow Down

Throughout the winter, I missed all the cues that should have alerted me to the peril building in Becca. She continued to mention the tingling in her hands and feet, and I continued to ask if she was scheduled to see the doctor soon.

"Yes, I need to do that," she would say. The ambiguity of her response should have been an indicator to me that I needed to insert myself more forcefully. Instead, I second-guessed myself and wondered if she wanted space. "I need to slow down," was the only thing I really heard.

I have let many significant moments slip through my fingers. More to the point, I have let them go unexamined. They were an opportunity for me to slow down and feel what was going on around me—and maybe even learn something. I quickly pushed past many heavy situations as I kept racing through life in a hurry to show up for everything and everyone.

Mount Baker Ski Area in Washington State broke the world record for snowfall during the winter of 1998–99 with 1,141 inches. On Saturday, February 14, 1999, I went to Baker with my brother, Blake. It had

Opposite: What goes up in deep snow comes down in deep snow. Two Mount Baker riders putting in the work to reap the benefits. Washington. *Colin Wiseman*

snowed a foot the night before, as had become an almost nightly standard that year. Getting on one of the first chairs, we rode powder inside the ski area boundaries all morning. In the afternoon we decided to go for a hike up a ridge known as Shuksan Arm, into the backcountry. I was in a hurry, but I waited for Blake while he gently wiped his goggles down and tied his jacket around his waist. Still waiting, I said hello to a pair of skiers who had just arrived and were beginning to prepare for the hike as well.

All four of us were ready at the same time. The steep climb is kicked into the snow, and the result is a rough stair-like path with an incline similar to a ladder and single file only. I did not want to feel the pressure of having someone hiking behind me, so I politely suggested to the others that they go first. A few minutes later, Blake and I began our climb.

After that first steep section, the path leveled out along the ridgeline. At this point the two of us hiked side by side, with Blake filling me in on what his first year of college was like. The surroundings were quiet and beautiful, with glaciated Mount Shuksan towering above. I noticed the two skiers ahead putting their jackets on and preparing to drop in. I suggested to Blake we go at least as far as they had and possibly drop in there also.

Blake and I kept walking and watched as the pair rolled into thigh-high powder and disappeared into the steepness. Then I heard a heavy boom. It was a crushing sound so great it produced a shock wave. Then a blast of icy wind pushed forcefully up the left side of my face. Turning my head left, looking over the drainage below, I saw snow blowing straight up, then curling away. It was exactly like offshore winds blowing water droplets up a wave face.

The wind stopped almost as fast as it began. Silence. For an instant I thought everything was normal, and looking down at my left boot I was confused about what I saw. All of the snow had broken away right up to my boot and now there was a steep mountain face, where before had been a flat field of snow. I looked behind me to see much of the trail we had just walked was gone, fallen into the valley below. "We aren't going back the way we came," I said to Blake. "We are riding out of here now!"

We began to buckle into our boards, looking down into the valley to find a safe line out. A crowd had gathered below, at the start of our hike, just inside of the ski area boundary proper. Staring at the group, I watched as they began to wave ski poles in the air, and then I heard them shout in unison, "NO!" Apparently, the pitch below was unsafe. I later learned it had not completely broken away in the initial event and the hangfire still clung unstably to the mountainside. Had we dropped there like we intended, we would have likely triggered another slide.

Hiking much farther out, we found a new spot and waited to see if the crowd below waved us off again. Their silence gave us the green light. Emotionally spent, we snowboarded down and across a gigantic avalanche debris field. I thought of the two skiers who began their descent just minutes before the valley was wiped clean. Feeling small and insignificant, I saw full-grown fir trees snapped in half like matchsticks. The snow didn't look like snow at all, but more like photos of moonscapes I had seen as a child. The snow felt hard and gravelly under my board, like asphalt.

One of those skiers died that day, and the other narrowly escaped with his life. I would learn much later that the avalanche had been ranked as one of the largest in history. The following year the ski area implemented a backcountry requirement that includes not only a partner, but also a beacon, probe, shovel, pack, and knowledge of how to use the gear correctly.

A brief exchange of politeness was all that separated those skiers' fate from mine that day, but I never took the time to let the weight of that thought sink in. I thought about that avalanche a lot during the moments I tried to understand how I could slow down for Rebecca. It was a moment where I should have paused and slowed down to appreciate the fragility of it all. But I just kept going, telling myself that life is a gift and that I need to show up and get back in the arena after every close call.

That avalanche was a chance for me to slow down, share the experience, and benefit from taking a moment to feel the emotions coming from a brush with death. There have been so many circumstances of rare odds in my life, yet I have raced through them without examination. Other people close to me had told me to slow down at different points in my life as well, not just Rebecca.

I went over another moment in my mind when I should have learned something, but didn't. As I did so I started feeling guilty, not because of what happened back then, but because I desperately hoped I could slow down for Rebecca. *Would I ever get the point?*

Rebecca has been rushed through many important moments of her life since meeting me. I regret this. For the most part, though, my energy and constant drive to do more in life has been a positive thing for us. Still, I remember times as a young couple when she would say, "Let's not worry about the next house, and just enjoy living in this one right now." Or moments when she was tired of my panicking about surf and would say, "Don't tell me the report, just tell me when we are leaving and where we're going, okay?"

As a kid I had begun to make decisions about life based on the motto "I had to go to know," and so I should "go" every chance I got. Later, I added "go for it" to the phrase and reminded myself that not only do I need to "go to know," but also I needed to "go for it" as well.

Over a lifetime, my mantra just grew until my approach more accurately could be found in the statement, "You have to go, go, go, go, go, go, go, to know."

Rebecca began to ask me to slow down a little and then a little more. Confused at first and then worried, I believed my pace had relaxed with the loss of vision. But pace is a relative thing, as is patience and gentleness. One of the most important challenges of our life was coming, and it would command that I slow down, pay attention to what Becca needed, and share in her emotions.

Opposite: Rebecca, strong and beautiful on the beach in Baja, Mexico. 2017.
Madrona Raney

CHAPTER 13

I Have Run as Far as I Can Go

That December we drove to Bend, Oregon, for the Dirksen Derby. Madrona did well and I put my energy into snowboarding as a family. Back home, I rode with Madrona on every powder day and didn't think about much else.

In January, Rebecca saw a physician recommended by her ob-gyn. Since moving to Bainbridge four years earlier, Becca had not been able to find a doctor on the island, so she was glad for the referral despite the hour's drive to the new doctor's office. However, she was discouraged when she left the appointment fifteen minutes later. At home, as I pressed for details, Rebecca said, "It was not a good fit. The woman did not take me seriously. Almost immediately she tried to put me on antidepressants and then told me I was not taking care of my body. It was over in ten minutes, and we never broached my main concern about what could be causing the tingling in my hands and feet." A search for a more supportive doctor-patient relationship continued, but without the urgency it deserved.

As always, we spent as much time at Baker as possible. There were moments that felt light and joyful, but it was becoming a more common occurrence for Rebecca and me to find ourselves in frustrating interactions because our communication was off and we didn't understand why. On a solid powder day, the two of us argued heavily as we hiked out of a drainage section we rode often. The argument seemed to be about the difficulty Becca was having as she booted out the powder and how I chose the wrong route out. I was looking for the connection the two of us always used to find in the snow, but our interactions made me want to quit snowboarding.

Madrona continued to rip and seemed not to notice the frustrations her mom and dad were having. She competed that month in the Locals Banked Slalom, which was the qualifier for kids to enter the Legendary Banked Slalom in February. She made the cut and began looking forward to the big event.

Becca remained tired, and it was all too easy to blame the fatigue on stress. In mid-January, our business entered a crucial stage in our coffee shop rebrand project. It was imperative that we make final decisions and adhere to the schedule that we had set. If we did not manage this time period efficiently, we would not make our target date of March 4, 2016. This was the day our new signs needed to go up and the old signs come down. After twelve years, we were changing the name of our shop to YES Please! Coffee. Wanting to stay current and say something about who we are as people—regardless of the turmoil we felt—we wanted to show our focus would always remain on saying "yes." Yes to each other, to life, to change, and to challenges.

In February, Madrona was on the podium at the Baker Banked Slalom. Tom Burt and his daughter Nina stayed with us at our cabin for four days during the race. Becca loves being around Tom, and watching her talk with him, smiling and engaged while they worked together in the kitchen, I thought our rough patch was over and the memories of Mexico were fading.

I was excited about the on-site construction aspects that would be a part of the next few months. I believed this was a chance for me to really support Becca. Working together on a project like this was what we were good at. Instead, I felt like I was in the way, and I soon became alarmed at how off our rhythm really was.

Repeatedly, I would say things like, "What? We have never done it like that," or "You know that's not how it works," or "Let me call him. That's my job."

Everything I said was insensitive and made her feel small. At the same time, I didn't recognize the person I was working alongside, and it scared me. It was during that time I first heard her say, "My memory is off."

"I don't remember what happened," she'd say. Confused, I believed she didn't want me involved in the process or managing the construction side of things. I had no visual of her face and couldn't see her pain or how tired she looked. We existed in silence and absence; often she chose to sit across the room instead of right next to me. It was the loneliest time of our lives.

After the new signs went up, our focus turned to the future. Becca was excited to move forward. The new name, YES Please! Coffee, held a strong sense of pride for both of us, not only because of what it said about us, but also because of what it said about the way Rebecca operated the business. With the future in front of us, it felt like a good time to try and slow down. Again, I wondered what that meant exactly and looked for ways to lessen stress in our world.

The months following our opening—March, April, and May—Becca began to get sick with common colds and headaches every other week or so. Tired, she would sleep fifteen hours a day. Both of us began to realize something was not right, and then blamed it on stress. I hoped sleep would help her manage.

Showing up every day to be a part of Becca's life was the one thing I was sure I knew how to do. But it was not as easy as simply showing up in the physical sense, because my eyes kept me from seeing the pain on her face, the circles under her eyes, and the weight she had lost.

During the spring, I pulled out the weeds and turned over the soil in the garden beds Rebecca and I had spent years building and maintaining. I left the kitchen door open as I worked, the open door an invitation—more like a plea—I hoped Rebecca would recognize. But she never came out. I planted the beds with the usual variety of tomatoes that Rebecca had planted all the years before. Her tomatoes were a summer highlight for all of us, and as I stood by myself looking around at what I had planted, it became obvious by her absence that whatever was going on with Rebecca was serious. Rebecca loved working with her hands in the yard,

Opposite: With beautiful form, Madrona makes one of her finishing turns to get her on the podium with a second-place in-category finish at the 2019 Legendary Banked Slalom. She was amazing to watch. Mount Baker, Washington. *Kevin McHugh*

caring for every living thing, and finding some time alone in the process. But she didn't work in the garden at all that summer, and later, when I brought ripe tomatoes inside to eat, they didn't have the flavor or size they would have if Rebecca had tended their vines. Even the vegetables missed her.

Showing up began to mean that I needed to insert myself in ways I had not done previously. "Have you found a new doctor? Are you still feeling the tingling? You should take a trip with your friends."

Rebecca took a trip with her four close friends to New York in May. There, she was able to relax and fully share what had been going on with her. Her tremors were so bad during the trip that her friends convinced her she needed to see a doctor. One friend suggested Becca see a functional medicine specialist who had helped her. At the end of June, Rebecca would have her first appointment with Dr. Gillian Ehrlich in Seattle.

In June, we left for Cabo San Lucas for an extended family vacation with Becca's parents, Larry and Robin Storset. They had reserved a three-bedroom time-share condo on a beach with three fantastic surf breaks right out front. Becca, Madrona, and I were all stoked to be going, and none of us spoke about our last Mexico trip.

Becca's folks picked us up at the airport and drove the short distance back to the resort. Madrona went straight for the pool with her grandparents, who had already been there for a week and knew the layout. Becca and I walked out to the beach. The familiar franticness associated with good surf was everywhere, and I could hear well-spaced sets peel perfectly along the reef and crash up the steep beach. We hurried back to the condo, where I unpacked my boards and learned they had been damaged in flight. They were both useless, and walking back to the beach I became anxious because I was missing good surf.

The two of us walked the beach for a bit and then sat down on the edge where the sand dropped off steeply. I began to grumble some standard complaint about how it sucked to not be surfing, when Rebecca cut me off and in seconds, I was no longer thinking about riding waves.

"I need to tell you something," Becca said with a tremble in her voice. Crying at first, and then shaking as I tried to hold her, she began to scream. "Don't! Just listen. I need you to just listen."

Between tears, she said that something was wrong with her mind.

"It's been going on for a while, and sometimes I have horrible thoughts," she said. "A few times I have wanted to die, but then I think of Madrona. After a while something changes and I can see how crazy my thoughts were, but the bad ones last for hours. I know something is wrong; I can feel it. It's as if I feel like I might be dying, and I spend a lot of time going over the way I should prepare Madrona for when I am gone."

Then she cried with a force I had never seen. I wish I could say I did something—anything—that I became her Knight in Shining Armor. I did not. After a feeble attempt to get close again, it was clear she wanted me at arm's length, and so I continued to sit motionless.

Becca continued by saying she had come to believe a force existed that was working against us. "We're under attack all the time," she said. "Too many hard things, and too many crazy things, have happened to us."

"We have accomplished so many amazing goals," I countered as I spoke for the first time. "I know at times we have lived too fast, and also that we've taken on a lot of risks as young people, but they have definitely had their rewards." She didn't seem to hear me, and I tried again by saying, "With all the adventure we have had, the odds are high that occasionally something bad will happen."

"Don't try to convince me," she said. "This is not an argument. I need you to listen. Please just listen," and then she reminded me of things I had forgotten about.

"Do you remember when we were hit by that drunk driver on the freeway Christmas night? You were driving the van, Madrona was a baby, and the car flipped upside down from oncoming traffic and hit us head-on!" she shouted. "I don't know anybody who has been in a wreck like that.

"And I don't know anyone who has been robbed in Mexico while they were sleeping," she said, and I could hear in her tone that she was beginning to calm. "And why can't we have more kids?" she asked as she let out a small cry. "We have been trying for so long.

"I know something is wrong right now. I need you to be patient," she said over and over, "and gentle. Don't try to fix this and don't try to fix me." The words hurt more every time she said them. "Please be patient, please be patient," was all she continued to say.

Exhaustion took over, and it became the right moment for me to sit closer and put my arms around her. But I remained frozen in the sand. It was my chance to tell her that it was temporary, that all of her bad thoughts and emotions would pass and soon we would be through this. It was my chance to prop her up and carry her like she had done so many times for me. But I didn't. I just sat there.

That moment will haunt me always. It was the greatest failure of my life. Actually, I consider that entire week to be the greatest failure of my life.

I spent the rest of the week thinking about myself, not Rebecca—there is no other way to put it. My pity party seemed to go on forever as I wondered how I would find patience and gentleness, two traits I did not naturally have. Traits that had served me well were now pushing Becca away, and I was becoming more concerned about losing her than drawing her near. A strong will, stubborn spirit, and tenacious approach were going to push away the one I loved. Even if those thoughts hurt and were focused on us as a couple, it was still about me and not her. At that moment, I realized I had run as far as I could go. If a bottom existed, I had hit it.

Rebecca had run as far as she could go as well, but it was not clear to us yet why she had hit bottom or what we were going to do.

The following weeks at home were the hardest, and I learned I could fall even lower. My eyes continued to block me from seeing the facial cues of just how much pain Becca was in. We spent the evenings sitting in bed together, going to bed much earlier than normal, hoping to talk, and then mostly sitting in silence. I would glance over at her, and then spend the time wondering how she was unable to see herself the way so many people viewed her. I was trying to understand what was going on in her mind, and I had very little to go on as we spoke less and less. I concentrated my energy by making mental lists of all the ways Becca was amazing. This was my tool so I wouldn't forget who she truly was, and any chance I got, I reminded her by reciting something from that list.

Still, I showed my lack of patience and gentleness in our arguments. Often, a small thing would derail a discussion, and I would get so confused by what we were talking about that anger would set in. Rebecca would retreat, and I would feel like a failure again.

Many times I would turn in for the night and find Becca sitting in bed rereading our old blog, Bikes, Boards, Blind, on her laptop. She would say, "It was such a happy time." While I agreed, and was glad she had the tool to jog her memory, I was nervous because I had no big adventure planned that could recapture that joy we felt. Even if I did, I didn't believe it would fix what was going on.

I was frantically searching for patience and gentleness. I forced myself to find ways to keep Becca at home, resting or at least not using up her time on me. I vowed to never ask Becca for a ride again. I hired Nick Fleming, our neighbor, a high school senior. He started working for me on a set hourly schedule during the summer. We worked on projects at our coffee shop, and we drove to the surf when it was good.

I asked Rebecca to walk with me on a daily basis, to and from the closest beach to our house. Rain or shine, I would carry blankets or whatever we needed, and together we made the three-mile round trip almost every day. I had decided that I would learn patience and gentleness by stubbornly forcing myself to acquire them. Or at least that is what I told myself so that I could maintain hope. Eventually, they would come to me. During our walks, I asked Rebecca a lot of questions so I could get her talking. Patiently, I would try to listen and not fix anything.

During Rebecca's first appointment with Dr. Ehrlich, it became clear that Becca had found a good fit. Dr. Ehrlich took her time, focused on Rebecca's tingling, and worked to peel back the layers of Rebecca's individual biology. At no point was a prescription considered as a quick solution. Instead, Ehrlich ordered Becca to the lab for some basic blood work. A follow-up appointment was scheduled to discuss the results.

At home we did some research, since we had a better understanding of what her symptoms were. Much of what we found compared her symptoms to that of early-onset dementia. I lived in a dark place, thinking about losing my partner to that horrible ailment.

Throughout that entire summer, no matter how tired she was, or how sick she felt, Rebecca was available for Madrona. We did

our best not to alarm Madrona, and we didn't have any hard data or firm results yet; still, Madrona knew her mom wasn't feeling well and often made dinner or brought her soup in bed. But for all the moments when Becca was low, I was always surprised at how resolutely she could be present when Madrona needed her.

Our Boston Whaler was in a boat slip at a marina not far from our house. The two of us would walk to the marina and Becca and I spent many hours sitting in the boat, not going anywhere, just talking. Often I wanted to take the boat out for a ride and leave the dock, but Rebecca just enjoyed sitting in the sun, and so we stayed put. I was beginning to understand the ways I could show up emotionally, by listening to what she said and truly hearing what she meant. It was rare when I got things right, but I felt a sense of growth when I did.

Rebecca had her follow-up appointment with Dr. Ehrlich in August. The general panel of results showed low levels in alarming areas like iron. Dr. Ehrlich told Rebecca that some of her levels were low enough to warrant further blood work, which would show more detail. In particular, the new panels would test her levels of B12, which supports the human nervous system.

On September 2, Rebecca went in to see Dr. Ehrlich again. "Your B12 is nearly depleted and because your symptoms are so profound, it is most likely chronic, as these low levels must have existed for some time," Ehrlich said. "This is something we need to fix. I want to try to bring your levels up with a series of B12 injections. And since the level is so low, I want to order a DNA test for a genetic disorder common in women of Scandinavian descent." The genetic test was ordered, and we played the same waiting game we had become familiar with during the pursuit of my diagnosis.

During this time, Rebecca went to Madrona's school for parent-teacher night to learn what Madrona's upcoming year would look like. The school is located across the street, less than a block away. In the classroom, listening to the orientation, Rebecca looked around and couldn't remember where she was.

Opposite: On the beach with Rebecca trying to stay warm ... and learn a little patience as well. Bainbridge Island, Washington. 2016. *Jeff Hawe*

The memory loss continued for the whole hour of the presentation, after which she had found her truck, but couldn't figure out what to do from that point. It felt like eternity until everything came back to her.

In October, Rebecca was diagnosed with methylenetetrahydrofolate reductase. Like Dr. Ehrlich had suspected, Becca had a genetic disorder, or mutation, more commonly known as MTHFR. MTHFR blocked her body from absorbing the vitamin B12. Often the genetic disorder can appear after trauma or shock, but there was no way of knowing how long her levels had been depleted. Rebecca would tell me later that she felt something happening in her body even before our ill-fated trip to Mexico. Still, for Rebecca, it was the best-case scenario in my opinion.

She learned that the low levels of B12 had caused the tingling sensation in her hands and feet. Her symptoms were extreme and most likely the result of the extended time period Rebecca had been living with such depletion. The horrible thoughts, delirious moments, and memory loss, which had been causing her to live in a prison of solitude, had also been the result of the chronic depletion. Later, when she met a few others with the same disorder, they had all experienced similar things.

She would raise her B12 levels by giving herself injections of a premeasured dose of the vitamin. Becca was told she needed to inject the serum three times a week until she could begin a once-a-month larger dose considered the maintenance shot. Doctors, researchers, and people we met with the same disorder said that her memory would return to normal, the tingling in her hands and feet would go away, and the thoughts of delirium would disappear.

We both have genetic disorders, I thought when I heard the news. I did not share the thought with her; it would take some time before I cracked any lighthearted jokes. The first time I heard the acronym for hers, MTHFR, I laughed out loud thinking that's exactly what our year was: a Mother F*****. Turns out, the other women Becca knew with the disorder had all made that same joke.

Before we received the result, we had already agreed to stay in Washington during October, instead of heading south like we usually did. It was an intentional effort on my part to be patient and slow down. Although I still wouldn't claim to be a patient

Rebecca and her YES Please! Coffee team members during one of her Latte Art Throwdowns. Port Orchard, Washington. 2016. *Raney Family Collection*

person, I had grown a little by that point. Laughter showed up again in our lives, and home was feeling like a good place to be. With time, Becca's energy level came up to its normal state, and she hasn't been sick or run down since. No electric hands, no bad thoughts, and her memory is getting better as well.

I watched as Rebecca's general health improved almost instantly after she began the injections. But her confidence was slower to return. Often she seemed to second-guess herself, and I figured this was because of the memory loss she had experienced.

On our walks I would ask her, "What makes you feel the most confident right now?"

"Working at the shop with the girls," she would say every time. "I remember everything there, and I like my leadership role."

When she was wearing her business-owner shoes, it was confident Rebecca all the way. So I tried to pump her up all the time.

"You empower those ladies," I would say. "They want to be you," I would go on. "You have employees that have been with you for twelve years," I said. "Don't forget how committed you are to the craft of coffee. You are loyal, have integrity, get all your ingredients in Washington, and you are still the only game in town committed to local dairy," I boasted for her.

She would reply, "Stop blowing smoke—nobody is as great as you make me sound."

Both of us would laugh and then I would start again. "You know, I have met a lot of professional women, and you truly are the real deal."

I had relied on more than just Becca during those early days of my vision loss. Friends and family helped restore my confidence during that time. I had the same hope for Rebecca. However, both of us did very little sharing of our struggle during the time she was sick. We were both fearful of becoming the couple who had yet another problem.

I was landscaping at our shop when I was approached by one of Rebecca's most senior employees, who I knew well. Amanda had been working at our shop for over ten years. "How is Rebecca feeling? She was sick a lot this summer, and I just wanted to ask you if everything is all right," she said. I took the opportunity and told Amanda everything.

Later, sometime in mid-November, my phone rang. "Hi, Devon, it's Jessie." Jessie was a past employee, now a mother of three and someone Rebecca still stayed in touch with. "We have all been working on something for Rebecca and I would like to bring it to you."

Jessie drove out to Bainbridge a few days later, picked me up, and we went for coffee. "This is what me made," Jessie said at the table as she handed me a thin bound booklet of essays. "Twelve of us, past and present employees, have written our thoughts and feelings on why Rebecca matters to us."

"Wow," was all I could say. Jessie read a few to me over coffee and it was hard not to get choked up.

The book, which they had put together beautifully, is a compilation of testimonials that showed the many ways Becca had empowered them as women and influenced their lives as people. The common thread I noticed, touched upon by all, is Rebecca's ability to lead by example. After they gave it to her, it would be months before Rebecca could read any part of the book without bursting into happy tears.

On December 19, fourteen months after being robbed in Mexico and six months after that horrible day on the beach in Cabo, Becca and I celebrated our seventeen-year wedding anniversary. That year life had reminded us—like it had many times before—that we are entitled to nothing, but we reminded each other that our walk through life is done together. Life is meant to be experienced, and to do this we have to go to know, and show up for each other every day, not just physically, but emotionally as well.

On our anniversary, we took wine and treats down to the shoreline in Eagle Harbor on Bainbridge. Our boat was out of the water, since it was December, and so I brought plastic yard chairs. I uncorked the wine and handed Becca a glass. "I need a blanket," she said, and so I handed her one of the Mexican blankets I had brought. I poured some wine into her glass and put my cold hands back into my jacket pockets.

"This was the toughest year of my life," I tried to say casually.

"How was it harder than those first years of your eyes?" she asked.

"Because during that time I got out of bed every day for you, and for our family. But it never occurred to me that something new might come along and take you away, and I wouldn't be able to do a thing about it."

"Cheers," she said, and drank her wine. It was the most significant mile-marker of our marriage.

"It's snowing at Baker," I said. And the following day we went snowboarding together.

CHAPTER 14

Ride Powder With Family and Friends

"We're broke again," Becca said with a laugh, and I knew instantly she was not really freaked out. It was not a "we are broke" in a burn-the-furniture-for-heat type of way, but rather a we'll-be-eating-quesadillas-until-I-can-put-more-money-in-the-account type of way. It was January 2017.

We were in our cabin at Mount Baker for the extended weekend, like usual, except the Locals Qualifier for the upcoming Legendary Banked Slalom would be held on that Monday, January 16. Madrona was racing and hoping to qualify for the big race in February.

It had been a little over a month since Rebecca and I celebrated our seventeen-year anniversary, and nearly four months since she began injecting the B12 serum. The important things, hope and laughter, were with us again, and Rebecca was strong and energetic. Still, I went over to see what monetary concern most alarmed her. "Where does it all go?" she said rhetorically.

"Why are you doing that now?" I asked.

"I was just looking at our accounts; you know I'm always looking," she stated.

"What is our biggest expense?" I asked.

She laughed. "Health insurance. Our premium is almost as much as our mortgage," she said.

I thought about this for a minute. "We could just drop it," I said in a deadpan tone. "You know how easy it is to be a dirt bag,"

Rebecca, beautiful as ever in the Mount Baker backcountry, Washington. 2017. *Raney Family Collection*

I continued, teasing. "Do you remember my visit to the gynecologist, after our first date?"

"That was not our first date. And why did you have that knife anyway? And why did I keep going out with you, is the real question," she said, laughing.

I didn't truly become a snowboarder until I moved to Washington State at the age of twenty. I had tried snowboarding a few times in California, on the hard pack at Mammoth and Mountain High. However, the first time I rode the deep powder in Washington, the sport seemed to bridge the gap between surfing and skateboarding for me. I was hooked for life, and in those early days I did whatever it took to snowboard as much as possible, no matter the cost or consequence.

Buying a pass was paramount for me, and it had to be purchased in the spring to capitalize on the reduced Early Bird price. Once my pass was purchased, I dealt with the rest of my finances on a day-to-day basis—more commonly known as the hand-to-mouth program.

Washington resorts are minimalist and quaint, without heated sidewalks, fancy restaurants, or slope-side stores selling Prada and Gucci. This fact and the old-style feel helps keep ticket prices down and is one of the reasons the sport of snowboarding remains financially accessible to so many folks in the Pacific Northwest today.

In the late 1990s I had a pass each year at Crystal Mountain. The lodge at Crystal had a cafeteria with a condiment bar to serve the patrons who purchased burgers. Their condiment bar was the swankiest around and kept me fed for free. On most days my lunch consisted of tomato slices, saltine cracker packs, and ketchup packets. The combination created healthy little sandwich bites, and I washed it all down at the drinking fountain.

Luxuries like car insurance and health insurance barely entered my mind.

In the summer, on one of our first unofficial dates, Rebecca and I went with some friends on a canoe trip. Borrowing her dad's Coleman canoe, we departed from Sunrise Beach, just north of Gig Harbor, and paddled two miles across the stretch of water known as Colvos Passage. We paddled for three hours and, arriving at Vashon Island, we pulled our canoe up a sandy stretch of beach and prepared to make a fire. Getting to work, we loosely set up our unsanctioned campsite. Vashon is the largest island in Washington's southern Puget Sound region, and without a bridge, it can only be accessed by boat or ferry. Most of the development on Vashon is either centrally located or on the eastern shoreline. I noticed with fondness how beautiful the summer sunset was as I gathered wood for our fire along Vashon's western edge.

Recently I had purchased a pocketknife. The knife had very little practical use, but it looked super cool, or so I thought. I would whip it out constantly, using a technique of aggressive wrist flicking, and brandish the blade with a speedy snap. Most often the knife was used to cut cheese for quesadillas. This was a go-to meal for me, especially when sleeping on the beach. Tortillas and cheddar are an easy combo to pack and don't require refrigeration.

Since I was on a date (I was beginning to consider it somewhat official) and wanted to impress Rebecca, I could have picked up twigs, but I chose to cut little wood shavings with my modern cowboy knife. These shavings, I said, "will really get the fire going." Then I smiled as I said, "We need a hot fire for those quesadillas I am going to make you."

Moments later I cut my hand. It was a nice-size gash over the top of my paw and into my knuckles. Most likely the cut came as I whittled the wood we needed to start our driftwood fire. However, I should mention that it is possible the laceration was the result of me constantly flicking the blade open and recklessly playing with the thing. The blood was flowing freely and I needed a bandage. Since I'd only brought cheese, tortillas, a wool sweater, and a sleeping bag, it was time to improvise. Looking super cool, I used my knife to cut a strip of cloth from my shirt, which I obviously had to remove as part of the process. Standing shirtless and using my survival tool to shred me off a bandage, I was sure I was impressing my lady as I attempted to save my own life. Probably, though, she was anything but impressed as I said out loud, "This better stop the bleeding, because I don't have health insurance."

Four of us slept that night under the stars and next to a beach fire. Since we were trespassing and a tent would indicate an obvious campsite, we lay in our sleeping bags exposed to the elements. This was almost always how our adventures went, and as a result we enjoyed a night in the rain.

The weather came in late. When I felt the drops on my face, I awoke and went through a few options in my head that might impress Rebecca as I tried to think up a dry solution. My thoughts were interrupted almost immediately, though, as I remembered the bandage wrapped around my hand and felt the painful ache from the evening's wound. I looked over at Rebecca where she lay on the other side of where the fire had been and saw that she was still sleeping. So I closed my eyes and tried to push the pain away. Unable to fall back asleep, I began to get the nervous feeling a doctor's visit was in my future. This only made me more nervous as I went over the recent course of events that left me uninsured.

That previous winter, I had decided to take a hard look at my finances. Sitting down, I focused on a budget, and gave it the full ten minutes I knew the job deserved. Inputting numbers on the balance sheet while doing some basic math, I said to myself, I am not working enough hours at the snowboard shop to cover my expenses.

When the summer returned I would be working construction again, but during the winter I was working part time at Northwest Snowboards.

Realizing my predicament, I had the obvious thought, If I increase my work hours, I won't be able to snowboard as much. *With a quick glance, I saw the big numbers in my expenditure column were in the line items of health and car insurance. So, with slight reluctance, I decided to stop payment on the insurance policies in an effort to keep current on the more necessary obligations like food, snowboards, skateboards, and gas to fuel my Volvo, which at the end of the month would be uninsured and illegal.*

I rationalized my choices by telling myself that my passion for snowboarding supports a healthy mind and body. In this way, I figured I probably didn't need that much health insurance anyway. I also promised myself that I would park my car for a while and get rides everywhere. However, soon I was reminding myself how safe a Volvo really was, and had convinced myself I didn't need car insurance for such a safe ride.

Budget is done, *I said to myself.* I'm off to the skate park.

Waking up in the rain, I realized I could not move the fingers of my left hand. As I pulled it up from inside my sleeping bag, I looked at a swollen hand now twice its normal size. Bright red and hot to the touch, so I spent the morning trying to keep the appendage hidden in my pocket. I rolled my sleeping bag up with one hand.

The following day it was even worse. It was hotter now, and achy, too, so I decided to show it to my dad. He called my mom in, and they said, "Ugh, looks infected." Appreciating their attention to detail, I said sarcastically, "Yes, it is. Any suggestions?" Looking at me now like it was a trick question, my dad said, "Might want to get some antibiotics."

Great, I thought. Now I am going to have to explain how my coverage disappeared after I did some personal downsizing to my health plan. *Knowing the whole truth had to be made clear, I said sheepishly, "I had to shore up my expenses, and health insurance has not been making the cut." I neglected to mention the part about car insurance not making the cut either.*

My folks were silent. They were not surprised. It was not the first time I had made a socially irresponsible decision to support my passions. Giving my situation some thought, my dad said frankly, "Our friend Bob is a gynecologist." As if that was all I needed to know, he finished with, "Mom can give him a call for you." Grateful, and assuming he would just call in some antibiotic, I said, "Thanks, Mom, let me know what to do." An hour later my mom said, "You have an appointment tomorrow at eleven 'oclock." *Forgetting to remain grateful, I said, "What? At the gynecologist's office?"*

In the morning I was on the brink of cancelling my appointment, but my hand continued to heat up and feel worse. So I got into my uninsured car and headed to my first-ever gynecologist appointment.

I entered the lobby cautiously and went to the receptionist. I began to speak, apparently too softly, because after two words the office worker yelled, "What?" Horrified that I had to speak louder, I replied, "I am here for my appointment at eleven with Dr. Bob." More calmly now, she looked at the computer, smiled, said, "Here you go, Devon," and handed me some paperwork. I was hoping to avoid any official record of my visiting a gynecologist, but I did not want to make a scene. I took the paperwork and sat down.

The form was actually going pretty well at first. I filled out my name, followed by my birth date. The next question was "How were you referred to us?" This seemed straightforward, and so I wrote, "My parents are friends with Dr. Bob." The fourth question was also a breeze: "Who is your insurance provider?"

Relieved that the questions were easy, I wrote, "Cash plan."

Section 2 of the form did not go as well. Labeled "Previous Gynecological History," the first question was "Do you have any pelvic inflammation?" Subconsciously I glanced down at my jeans, and thought, No, I am good. Looking ahead to the following question, I read, "Do you have any vaginal infections?" That was enough for me, and I turned the form in.

Eleven in the morning is apparently a busy time for gynecologists. I had originally hoped that I would be by myself in the lobby, but I wasn't. I was, however, the only man. As I looked around the room, I noticed that all the women had great posture, with their backs straight and stiff, their legs uncrossed, and their purses on their laps. The stiff backs looked uncomfortable to me, and I thought to myself, It's probably the pelvic inflammation. Soon I was called into an exam room.

When I entered the exam room I looked for a chair. The nurse motioned to the obvious choice, which was like a dentist's chair with foot rests. Looking at it with horror, I instead took a seat against the wall, in what I assumed was a chair meant for husbands who were brave enough to make it this far. The nurse asked, "What can we do for you?" Grateful that my visit had nothing to do with my pelvic region, I held up my swollen hand, saying, "I have cut my hand and believe it is infected." Then I explained my situation, about my parents knowing

Dr. Bob and the arrangement my mom made to get this appointment.
At which point she took my vitals, put some stuff on my cut, and told
me to hang tight. While she was gone, I took the liberty of opening a
few drawers and the cabinet. Satisfied things looked normal, I became
slightly confused when at the last second I found a headlamp, and said
to myself, Wow, I think I have one just like this. *Trying to push the*
thought What does he need a headlamp for? *out of my head, I scold-*
ed myself and sat back in my chair.

Dr. Bob showed up, took a look at my hand, and wrote me a pre-
scription for an antibiotic. He said, "I am sorry you had to go through
check-in. It's been busy, and I forgot to tell them you were coming."

Grateful that he noticed the awkwardness, I said, "Oh, no problem,
I was fine."

Hoping a rear exit or service door existed, I tried to keep from turn-
ing red after Dr. Bob escorted me back into the lobby and said, "Thanks
for coming, Devon. Say hi to your parents for me."

Damn it, *I said to myself as I walked out of the room.* Now all
these ladies know my name. *It was almost enough embarrassment to*
make me sign back up for health insurance right then and there.

Rebecca was still laughing at the memory. "Don't even joke
about canceling health coverage," she said.

For a brief time in my early twenties, I had made some irresponsible choices and was somewhat of a happy dirt bag as a result. Being a dirt bag was easy. The real work came a little later,
after Rebecca and I were married and our world became slightly
more complicated as our decisions now affected each other. As
life went on, our sphere of influence grew, and our decisions not
only impacted the two of us but had a ripple effect on the lives of
those around us. At the point we became parents, our most basic
decisions would have a lasting effect on our child. As our business
grew, so did our feeling of responsibility toward the well-being of
our employees.

Our commitment to staying on the snow grew and matured
over time as well. And we found more legal and responsible ways
to make the sacrifices necessary to follow our passions. During
our first two years of marriage, we bought passes at Alpental Resort because they offered the best college discount. It was crowded on weekends and not my favorite, but it was affordable. So,

Madrona has been raised on the snow. White Pass, Washington. 2005.
Raney Family Collection

Rebecca managed to always enroll in some sort of class just for the discount.

Throughout those early years of marriage, Rebecca and I consistently slept in the back of our Volvo or under the canopy in the back of our truck. We chased surf around the Oregon coast, snow throughout Washington, and adventure wherever we could find it. At some point during that time, the two of us had spent so many nights in the back of our truck that Rebecca finally said, "Did you know that we have not slept in our bed at home this year for more than eight consecutive nights?" Our bodies may have paid the price of many stiff mornings, but our pocketbooks stayed flush by avoiding those hotel rooms.

After Madrona was born, staying on the snow took even more intentional effort. White Pass Ski Resort offered very cheap family passes, and so we bought ours and began riding new terrain again. Soon the truck bed started feeling a little cramped, so we purchased a cabin in Packwood, Washington, located at the base of White Pass. It cost $40,000 and was the definition of rustic. At the time, a full-size diesel truck cost the same amount. Instead of a new work truck, we bought a beat-down cabin and went to work fixing it up. Rebecca and I left all of our snow gear at the cabin, and by doing this we forced ourselves to snowboard only at White Pass. It was a constant temptation of ours to follow the snow dumps and show up at whatever resort received the most snowfall from the previous night's storm. But after we became parents, the most affordable plan was to simply stay put and accept whatever conditions our current resort choice had received.

The biggest sacrifice of all came in the form of exhaustion. I would work all day at the job site, Rebecca would work the early shift as a barista, and then we would panic out for our cabin to arrive at midnight before every storm. It was not a new formula—I had plenty of friends on the same program—but still it felt like we were constantly driving as we worked hard to get in as many powder days as possible, keep a career, raise a child, and pay the bills.

As Madrona got older, the effort increased in intensity. I grew bored with the limited terrain of White Pass, so we sold the cabin. Since the time when Madrona was two years old, we have called ourselves locals at Mount Baker, Washington. During our first few years at Baker we became friends with a fantastic woman named Jan Owens-Larsen. Jan began renting us a cabin on a six-month basis. This allowed us to keep a place at Baker for the winter and leave our bedding and snow gear there as well. These days the formula is the same as it was at White Pass: We rush to get off Bainbridge Island and show up at Mount Baker the night before a big storm.

Keeping the passion alive and making sure Madrona got as much time as possible on the hill became harder as she got further into grade school. It became clear that not only were kids under pressure to receive validation through school, but so were the parents.

At the beginning of every school year, Rebecca and I would meet with Madrona's new teacher and explain how our kid's seat would be empty during the winter. I would explain the challenges that existed in our family's daily routine because of my vision impairment. I spent a good deal of time painting a clear picture of how I was unable to read to Madrona or help her with homework. I also spoke of the roles Rebecca and I now had and how it was now my job to be the caregiver at home. We have yet to meet a teacher who didn't fully support our family and understand our position.

Madrona missed a lot of school in winter and as her absences built up, the school would send a form letter home in the mail notifying us that our child had missed an above-average number of days. As parents, we were required to call in and excuse our child when she was gone. Once while doing this, I left the school a voice-mail saying, "Please excuse Madrona as she is snowsick." Weeks later, the assistant principal pulled me aside and said it was the funniest message she'd ever received. In moments like that, I am overcome with gratitude for all the support we have received from Madrona's school district. Over and over again, her teachers have empathized with our situation and respected our commitment to family unity.

The pile of absence notices has stacked up over the years, and I have saved them all so I can give them to Madrona someday when she is older.

During her fifth-grade year, Madrona rode fifty-five days of powder, many of them school days. It's not the missed days I am proud of but rather the effort we have made to truly find a way to teach her, influence her, and play with her by simply showing up and sharing our passion. I have occasionally struggled with our choice to take Madrona out of school so much. In those moments of doubt, I remind myself why we do it. Snowboarding together as a family has kept us connected.

We don't always need to go as a whole family to see the benefits of that strengthened connection. Rebecca and Madrona have shared their own mother-daughter bond through the sport. The two of them have been at every opening day at Mount Baker since Madrona was four. Rebecca watches the weather forecast as the season opener gets closer and then takes the day off. The two of them get up at 3:45 a.m., take the 4:30 boat off the island, drive up to Baker, and ride all day.

Madrona and I get our own one-on-one time together as well. Since Rebecca occasionally returns to Bainbridge Island for work-related stuff, Madrona and I are left at the cabin to fend for ourselves. This means we stand with our thumbs out on the 542 East in the town of Glacier and hitchhike up the road to the ski area. Every time we hitchhike I am filled with pride and thankful for Madrona and Rebecca, who have worked hard to figure out new ways to get things done while adjusting to a life they never expected.

My life has been built around the passions I fell in love with at a young age. Eventually, my memories of surf, skate, and snow all began to flow into one vast recollection. So many good times, life lessons, great people, close calls, feelings of achievement, and moments of physical joy have become intertwined; my mental highlight reel dates back more than thirty years. However, for the past ten years many of these memories were shaped by one significant gift I received from the sport of snowboarding. Maybe, in a way, it was not a gift, but more like a reward, because it took some effort to earn.

I was in the Baker parking lot when I got the call from my doctor informing me of my eye diagnosis. I was in the parking lot again the following day with my family, ready to snowboard. Since that time we have continued to show up at Baker as a family. Madrona loves the mountains, and we have been committed to bringing her up in the environment at Mount Baker no matter who gets diagnosed with what.

Personally, I have struggled more than I let on to find the same type of enjoyment I used to have back when I could see perfectly. Since my vision impairment, my body has felt beat up and broken at the end of a day of snowboarding. It is such a stark contrast to surfing, which always leaves me feeling strong and confident.

Even after I became proficient with the technique, after years of tandem snowboarding, following a rider down the hill still had a few impossible problems. I have never been able to stay completely clear of all the bumps, compressions, and variety of undulations that all good shredders recognize far in advance. My snow style has become stiff and rigid, because my body is now a full-time shock absorber as it sucks up everything I don't see and can't be ready for. This feeling has been constant and frustrating beyond belief, especially since my time on the snow has been so important to me.

The joy I find from snowboarding these days comes from one major reason, and she is worth every one of those frustrating moments, bumpy rides, and body-breaking falls. I am glad Madrona's passion is snowboarding and that the mountains are her favorite place to be. And I am happy that she has already found something she loves. Even bigger than that is the joy I get as I participate with her. So many times she sounded like an angel when she would say, "Dad, it is snowing at Baker. Are we going soon?"

Snowboarding has allowed me to participate on a daily basis in Madrona's life, and that is the most powerful gift I have received from a lifestyle outdoors. I use the technique Tom Burt and I developed to follow my daughter down the slopes at Mount Baker. When she was little it was easy, but she got fast quick, and soon she was looking over her shoulder to see if I was still there. Although I can't see her face from across the dinner table, I have countless memories of Madrona's powder turns because I have ridden so close behind her so many times.

Unlike soccer, volleyball, or even surfing, snowboarding is the one thing I can still do that keeps me off the sidelines and in the arena with my daughter.

As she gets older, Madrona is becoming more and more involved in the competitive side of the sport as a racer, and it's teaching her many of the same life lessons skateboarding and surfing taught me when I was her age. Often I've wondered if she would learn more about life with an introduction to the more common team sports. These concerns were silenced in January 2017.

In 2016 as a ten-year-old, Madrona competed in the Next Generation category of the Legendary Banked Slalom race. The category is for girls eleven and under, and she placed third. Standing on the podium, she received a coveted bronze duct tape trophy. It was fun to hear her name on the loudspeaker and our locals cheering for her.

The two girls who placed first and second in her category are both exceptional snowboarders and are part of a Whistler, British Columbia–based race program. Passionate and strong, they are highly skilled both on and off the course.

Watching their runs during the event that year, Madrona commented on both girls' form and efficiency. I could hear the drive in my daughter's voice that I recognized in myself when she asked me, "Dad, do I look like that?" Madrona was beginning to wonder if she could find the form and technique to reach the level those two girls were at.

Mount Baker gets a ton of snow, and Madrona loves riding the deep powder. It is her favorite thing to do. She doesn't have a coach, a team, or a race course to practice on. On the contrary, she often gets stuck guiding her dad around the mountain. With or without her dad she likes the deep snow, and all the powder has made her strong. If the powder gets tracked out, Madrona finds her buddies and cruises the jump runs until lift operators call last chair.

The following October, Madrona learned that she didn't requalify with her third-place finish. However, the two Whistler girls had kept their spots in the main event because of their gold and silver finishes.

After explaining to Madrona that the cutoff had been second place, I told her, "That is part of racing," and she understood. She would need to requalify by racing in the upcoming locals qualifier in January and place high enough to get a spot in the main event held in February. Since she was eleven years old, I figured she wanted to race in her category—the Next Generation 11 and Under Girls.

Then Madrona learned that both Whistler girls, whom she had come to regard as peers, had turned twelve. They would both be racing in the next category up, Junior 12 through 15 Girls.

I was surprised at how bummed Madrona was. "You mean I don't get to race against them again?" she asked. She paused a second or two. "I want to qualify in their group. Will Gwyn let me do that?"

"I don't know," I said. "But I'll ask."

At home on Bainbridge Island a few weeks later, just before I kissed her good night, Madrona expanded on her thoughts. She explained her desire to race with the group that pushed her last year. If she stayed in the eleven-and-under race, she wouldn't know if she had improved.

Her goal was to see how she stacked up against the two girls she considered the best. It felt easy to her to stay down in her age

Opposite: Oozing style, Madrona has always had a playful spirit on a snowboard. Mount Baker, Washington. 2010. *Tim Stanford*

group and probably get a trophy. "I want to race with my group from last year, Dad," she said. I kissed her, and went out of the room with a swollen heart.

She was beginning to see competition the way I do, and I agreed with her decision. The contest is within; she is really competing against herself. The trophy doesn't matter, and neither does beating people simply for sport. Madrona had set a bar, and now she wanted to know if she could get there. To do that she would have to race in a category where she was the youngest girl.

Christmas Eve morning 2016 brought cold temperatures and new snow to Mount Baker. The three of us got on one of the first chairlifts that morning. It was clear and cold, and Becca remarked on how beautiful it was, adding, "It has not been this consistent of a winter in a long time."

I replied, "Consistently fun," and the three of us laughed.

We buckled our bindings, and Madrona asked her mom to take a photo of her as she hit a nearby kicker. It had been growing in size with each night's new snow accumulation.

"Follow me, Dad," Madrona said. "But don't hit the jump behind me." She sent it, Becca got the shot, and then I heard the cry.

I recognized the serious tone in Madrona's voice as she started yelling, "It's an injury! It's an injury!" She knew something was really wrong.

We left immediately and drove to the hospital on Bainbridge Island. X-rays confirmed Madrona's left arm was broken in two spots. We then took her to Seattle Children's Hospital, where the doctor put a needle into her bones near the fracture, injected a numbing agent, reset the bones, and put a hard cast on Madrona's arm.

The doctor never told her not to snowboard, nor even suggested she take time off. I think he naturally assumed she wouldn't go back with a cast. Rebecca and I did not tell her what she should do either. The two of us waited to hear how she felt, and I knew Madrona's decision would be based on how bad she really wanted to snowboard.

She made her decision, we drove back to Baker, and the next day Madrona was riding fresh snow again. Becca cut and retrofitted an extra-large mitten that fit over Madrona's cast. The only concern I ever heard from Madrona was whether or not the cast would slow her down when she pulled out of the start shack on race day.

On the day of the Locals Qualifier, Madrona competed in the Junior Girls 12 through 15 category. I sat by myself under a fir tree just behind the rope lines of the course and held my phone. Becca remained up at the start shack so she could take a photo and call me the moment Madrona dropped into the course. When my phone rang, I stood up, saw a shape moving down the line, and yelled Madrona's name. She qualified and earned a spot in the main event.

That night, driving home, Madrona was disappointed in her time. "I felt faster than that, Dad," she said. Tears came to her eyes. "I need help. How do I learn to race gates?"

I was quiet for a few minutes. Then, as carefully as I could, I said, "Madrona, you are an amazing snowboarder. When I follow you around Baker it is nothing but fun. I watch you pursue your passion and today you qualified with a broken arm. Mom and I have always hoped you would grow up with heart and strength of character. Your character blew my mind today, and we were so proud to watch you follow your heart. Going after a challenge and not taking the easy path will take you farther in life than anything else. I've taught you everything I know. It's amazing watching you learn as much as you have without any gates to practice on."

Later in the drive, I said, "Madrona, you are the underdog. Many kids have a coach and travel around to races. It is better to be the underdog and ride powder with your family and friends. I believe you will find your racing magic. You can learn a lot by paying attention to great racers and how they make their turns. You have an awesome story this year. Everyone cheers for the underdog, and the underdog has the opportunity to surprise us all."

She didn't say much, but I could tell she was thinking about it.

I have never been afraid of my kid failing. Failure is part of life. Madrona will have many failures throughout her life, and hopefully she will develop a little grit as a result. It is the habit of taking the easy path that I have always been afraid of. Not just for Madrona, but for myself as well. It was a peaceful feeling watching her make the hard choice to race in a group she will have a tough time competing against.

Madrona is becoming her own person and, in truth, the woman she will be for the rest of her life. She is strong and beautiful. Rebecca and I showed up to be a part of her life every day, no matter how overwhelming the change around us felt. I like to think the effort helped shape her world. I am grateful for the countless hours we have spent snowboarding together and for all the memories I have of her sitting on the beach and cheering for me as I surfed waves. Bringing her up in this environment is one of the few things I have been absolutely sure of.

In February, Madrona competed in the big race. Although she qualified on Saturday, she did not place in the finals. Still, she was racing with her peers and exactly where she wanted to be.

Knowing Madrona and Becca are getting on a chairlift together so they can go make turns as mother and daughter is one of the best feelings I get today. I don't ask for much more.

Opposite: Rebecca leading Madrona out for their favorite backcountry run. Mount Baker, Washington. 2018. *Raney Family Collection*

CHAPTER 15

A 41-Year-Old
Sixth-Grader

In September of 2016, Madrona entered the sixth grade. It marked the last year of her primary schooling and the beginning of many things way too grown up.

Monday, April 3, 2017, was the start of her spring break. Many people in Washington use spring break as a way to say good-bye to winter by traveling somewhere warm. We stayed home because it was still snowing every day at Mount Baker.

One evening during our stay-cation, my mom stopped by our house and dropped off an old shoe box full of keepsake items from the year I was in the sixth grade. She had been saving the artifacts for thirty-one years, and the collection proved to be a surprise in more ways than one.

Later that evening, Madrona and I went through the stuff she called old. We found my sixth-grade class photo, a boomerang I made at Indian Guides, and a mesh hat with the name of the soccer team I was on that year. With a smile, I stared at the black hat and read the word "Spurs" and remembered how proud my parents were when I made the team.

Under the hat was a collection of first-place ribbons I won in swim meets. Madrona asked what a swim meet is, and then

Opposite: Happy, in the water where I feel least blind. Todos Santos, Baja, Mexico. 2016.
Colin Wiseman

Captain Madrona Raney. Puget Sound, Washington. 2016. *Rebecca Raney*

concluded that growing up on a swim team must be why I walk to our local pool several times a week. Her outdoor pool has been Puget Sound, and her diving board the bow of a Boston Whaler.

The time warp continued as we found a yo-yo and I realized I had completely forgotten that the toy even existed. Mine was in perfect condition and the old slipknot fit my middle finger like magic. Around the backyard fire that night, I showed off my rusty yo-yo skills and then let Madrona try. I watched as she floundered and could not bring the disk back up to her hand. Laughing, I said, "Guess Apple doesn't make a yo-yo app."

At the bottom of the treasure chest lay the crown jewel, a storyboard report from my sixth-grade year titled "Who Is Devon Raney." The autobiography depicted how I saw myself then, gave a list of my hobbies, and told of my plans for the future. The project was made on the timeless three-panel display board used in every grade-school science fair since the beginning of mankind. Glued onto the left panel was my personal summary, on the right was my hobby list, and in the middle was my photo collage.

Madrona and I listened as Rebecca read what I had said about myself when I was in sixth grade. Halfway through the introduction she broke out laughing, then turned to me and said, "You are a forty-one-year-old sixth-grader."

"Hold on, hold on," I interjected. "Let's take this thing out to the fire and read the rest there." Everyone liked this idea and Rebecca opened some wine while saying to Madrona, "Grab some food and blankets—this is going to be good."

I built the fire and sat back to listen to the crackle as it grew. Our backyard pit is a simple ornamental iron stand with a recycled stainless-steel washing machine tumbler nestled inside, and I can easily find the curved lip, which creates the opening at the top of the bin.

Waiting for Rebecca and Madrona to join me, I thought about the countless hours I have spent staring at fires. Beach fires, backyard fires, campsite fires, job-site fires, and indoor woodstove fires have been entertaining me for as long as I can remember.

Madrona sat down next to me, and with too much parental judgment in my tone I turned to her and said, "You know, Sweetie, I have probably spent more hours watching a good fire than I have a TV."

"OK, whatever, Dad," she responded in annoyance.

I laughed out loud, and continued to poke. "I'm just saying you should be careful of those screens, that's all." Rebecca came out and sat down just in time, and after hearing the tail end of my sentence, she sarcastically said, "Is Dad giving you his Cowboy TV lecture? Are we all watching another rerun of Cowboy TV?"

We all laughed, and then it was Madrona's turn to poke fun. She said, "Yeah, Dad, you watch too much Cowboy TV; you don't need to make a fire every night." I smiled brightly, but sat silently as I remembered building a beach fire with Rebecca on one of our first dates and telling her how a good friend of mine calls staring at a fire Cowboy TV.

I heard Madrona say, "Mom, keep reading Dad's report," and I turned my attention back to Rebecca. She had the report in her lap and, picking up where she'd left off, began reading again. In the section for sports and interests I talked about my new skateboard, and how I intended to focus on skating that year. In the next line, I wrote about my passion for the ocean and said, "I have been surfing for one year, and I need new equipment." Rebecca burst out laughing again as she turned to me and said, "Nothing has changed; you always need new equipment." And when she continued teasing me with, "Didn't you just get a new surfboard?" Madrona was laughing too.

For the conclusion of my sports and interests section, I'd attached a photo of myself holding my skateboard and wearing a pair of Vans Original high-tops. Stapled next to the shot was a receipt proving my recent purchase. Madrona noticed the shoes I was wearing in the photo, and soon Rebecca and I were the ones laughing as Madrona said, "Wait! Dad had those Vans?" Madrona was confused, believing the shoes she had just gotten for Christmas were a new release. Rebecca was laughing hard now and said, "I used to wear OP corduroy shorts, and you and your friends think those are new designs too." She finished with, "Man, we're sounding old, Devon."

The bulk of my personal summary was about family, friends, and loyalty. "I just want to make my friends and family laugh," I wrote, followed by, "Loyalty is important, and I am loyal to my friends."

Rebecca handed Madrona the report so she could look at the photos and make fun of my neon 1980s attire. There was an open seat next to me on our wicker sofa, and Rebecca came and sat down next to me and laid her head on my shoulder. I reached for a blanket, threw it over her legs, and then closed my eyes.

With my eyes closed, I heard my daughter say, "Dad, you are the same guy." And I understood what she meant. Still, looking at her I asked, "What makes you say that?" She answered, "You always talk about loyalty, and how important it is to have a passion." Pausing a minute, she finished with, "Oh yeah, and you make me snowboard in the rain." The three of us laughed at that and then agreed how snowboarding in the rain can be fun. The rain makes the snow slushy soft. Madrona continued talking about how much fun it is to carve a snowboard in slushy snow while I silently thought about loyalty.

Loyalty, as I see it, is the strongest currency I have ever known. Its value is traded in the form of our word, and its worth increases with time, as it becomes trust.

It took only a second for me to think about my bicycle trip to Mexico and the loyalty my close friends showed me when they didn't hesitate to join the adventure. I thought about other friends whom I've known almost my whole life, and my brother and sister, whom I've known from the beginning. I thought about how fortunate I am to have had mentors who have shown me a better way to do things, and I thought about my dad, who has been there for me every time.

Then I turned my head to the left and thought, *Devon, you have the literal definition of loyalty sitting right next to you.*

I heard Madrona say, "Mom, can I make some popcorn?" Rebecca responded, "Of course." And then Madrona stood and went inside to pop the kernels.

Rebecca sat upright and turned to me before she said, "What are you thinking about?"

Without hesitation I replied, "I am thinking about how proud I am to be your husband." A minute went by and then I said, "Thank you for being so loyal."

Rebecca reached over and grabbed my hand and then held it tight. We sat for a while staring at the fire, and I knew both of us were happy and enjoying the moment. As we waited for the popcorn, I looked over at her and said, "I don't think I could have done it any better with perfect vision." The tears began to form at the bottom of my eyelids, and soon I felt the first one roll down my cheek.

Rebecca knew what I meant and hugged me hard. With her arms around me, she whispered, "You couldn't have been a more amazing dad. We got what we got, and we followed our hearts."

I wiped my eyes with the back of my hand and cleared my throat. "We have been through a lot, but our girl is amazing. If I hadn't lost my vision, I might not have spent as much time with Madrona." I continued my thought, saying, "If my eyes remained perfect, I might have gotten lost in the hustle and our family would have suffered more."

"Maybe," Rebecca said, "but I doubt it." And then, "Madrona is amazing, though, that is for sure."

As Rebecca spoke, I couldn't help but remember what she used to say to me back when our marriage was beginning. During that time Rebecca would say to me often, "Our future is wide open, and we can do anything we want as long as we do it together." She was right, and as I sat next to her around the fire almost eighteen years later, her words felt powerful.

"I don't think I ever told you this," Rebecca said excitedly. "During parent night at Madrona's school, I heard her teacher talking to a group of moms about child development. I didn't hear it all, but what I did hear was that a child's personality or character is believed to be established or formed by the time they turn eleven."

She paused for a minute and then continued, "I looked up the topic online, and most research does show that a child has formed their character at a young age. I forgot about it until tonight when your sixth-grade report jogged my memory."

Then she laughed and said, "I guess you are the living proof we need, since you definitely developed your character by the time you turned eleven."

Both of us were laughing, and I didn't want the moment to end.

"I guess we did OK with Madrona then," I said.

"We sure did."

Then I put my arm around her while we waited for popcorn and watched a little more Cowboy TV.

Opposite: Stoked to hear the enthusiasm in my kid's voice. Gold Coast, Australia. 2018.
Rebecca Raney

Next spread: My two legs to stand on: Rebecca Michelle and Madrona Adelle. 2018.
Colin Wiseman

DEDICATION

For Rebecca Michelle and Madrona Adelle. You have my whole heart for my whole life.

The Why, the How,
and the Who to Thank

Rebecca put the wager down and I gave her my best poker face. "Are you serious?" I said.

"Yup, if you write a book I will do something big, really big."

"Like buy a house in Mexico?" I asked sarcastically.

"Maybe, you'll have to write it and see," she added.

"Fine, let's shake on it," I responded. *Maybe I will make her buy a motorcycle,* I thought as we continued walking home, *and then I can ride on the back.*

She could tell I was thinking about our new deal and she tried to hedge her bet by saying, "Oh yeah, you have to get it published, and you have to get a book tour."

"Oh, give me a break," I laughed. "Now you sound nervous with all these new rules you're adding."

I started writing that evening. At two in the morning I got into bed, hugged her and woke her up, and wryly informed her that I would be winning the bet. Madrona and I listened to Rebecca as she read us my first story that morning. It was nonstop laughs from both of them and then they wanted to know when I would write another one. It was spring of 2015.

"You write like people talk," Rebecca had said to me many times. She had also asked me to write a book many times. I knew she wanted me to put our story down on paper. She could see something in me that I didn't clearly see myself, and that thing was writing. But I didn't want to write a book, at least not at first. I knew that no matter how many funny stories I had, they would eventually run out, and then I would have to write the painful stuff.

Because I cannot see the screen or the keyboard, the actual writing presented significant challenges at the start. I was typing by feel, using the Braille bump on F and J to line up my hands. I remembered how to find the period and comma keys, but to this day I still can't find the quotations key. For this reason I wrote all my dialogue in capital letters using the shift key I was familiar with. Because I could not see the screen I often forgot to put a space between words or correctly lay my paragraphs out the way I saw them in my head. Every time I wrote a story it needed to be cleaned up, read for flow, and all the conversation needed to be pulled out of caps and surrounded by quotes.

Briefly, I considered installing a voice program on the desktop computer I was banging away on. But thinking about the robot voice reading my thoughts back to me for hours and hours on end was a depressing thought. I was never going to ask Rebecca to be my reader or edit my work. I didn't want her to regret the day she laid out the challenge. Still, I needed to find a way to read my words or more accurately hear what I had written.

I solved my problem by hiring Catharine Fleming, our neighbor. She was a freshman in high school and at first the task was simple: read to me what I had written and then come back the next day so we could do it again. It wasn't long before she was getting raises and additional responsibility. Soon she became simply "The Voice" I heard in my head when I started typing. Catharine would sit down in front of the computer and together we would clean up my punctuation, put the dialogue into quotes, fix any spelling. I would spend hours listening to her read my writing to me. Then we would correct the flow, trash whatever major portions we didn't like, make notes, and then I would write some more that evening after she left.

I like to think that, at least in a small way, a friendship was formed between Catharine and myself. I would look forward to the time we spent working because her steady narration skills made it easy for me to tell where I needed to clean up my storyline. Anytime she got hung up or paused, I would stop her from reading further and address whatever it was that caused her to fumble. Almost always it was my writing that needed the cleanup and not her narration.

Catharine entered her junior year of high school and we were still working, only now she had become a sounding board for the way I felt my themes were going to be received by the younger generation. For many reasons I should thank Catharine first. Without her I would not be writing a list of acknowledgments in the first place. When I think about how long it has taken me to write this book, and then think about how I could have listened to a computer-generated voice instead, I simply shiver. A human connection kept me going and for that I have Catharine to thank.

In June 2018 I received an email from Karla Olson, director of books at Patagonia, offering me a contract to purchase the rights to my book. I was with Tom Burt and we were headed out for a surf. I can still hear Rebecca's voice in my head as she chased us down the trail shouting, "Devon, you have an email you are going to want to read!" It was a significant moment.

I would like to thank Karla Olson for believing in me, inspiring me, and supporting my unique process. Also, thank you to everyone at Patagonia who put their touch on this book in some way or another and who make that company so amazing.

I would also like to thank John Dutton, the senior editor at Patagonia. It was an honor working with John. I knew of his work on the Patagonia project *180° South*, and from the start I was awestruck and a little intimidated that I was going to be working with him.

I do not have the words to properly thank Sarah Morgans, the editor who has worked alongside me for the past year. Sarah taught me how to kill my darlings, keep my voice without sounding like I love my voice, and that sarcasm is tough to convey in text. As with Catherine, our process was entirely conversational, with our discussing Sarah's suggestions, Sarah making the agreed-to edit in the document, and then reading through sections again so that I always kept my bearings as the narrative arc evolved.

I need to thank my parents, Dave and Pam Raney. If there is any hint of good writing in this book, it is simply because my mom made me read all the classics, as well as a million other books, and because of all the hours I spent watching my dad write.

Thank you to Colin Wiseman, Josh Dirksen, Jeff Hawe, and Kristin West for the right words at the right time.

I want to thank a group of friends and family who read to me around the fire many times over the years I spent doing this. Teresa Muehlenkamp, Scott Gravatt, Jeff Hawe, David Avice, Jason Dunham, Paavo and Jordan, Laura Raney, Dave Raney, Valerie Valk, and Rebecca were the fireside reading club.

A huge thank you to Kelda Jean Martensen for her commitment to representing my energy in her artwork.

Most of all I have to thank Rebecca—for everything. So many times throughout my writing process I felt like I was simply digging a hole then filling it back up, taking a step to the side and digging another hole so I could fill it in as well. In these moments I didn't know where I was headed or what I was truly doing. Rebecca seemed to always know and she actually enjoyed watching me work. So I kept digging and eventually we found the treasure when I held *Still Sideways* in my hand.

Following spreads:

Speaking at Bird's Surf Shed at the end of the Bikes, Boards, Blind adventure. San Diego, California. 2013. *Jeff Hawe*

With Tom Burt, and probably talking his ear off. In a minute he'll say, "Go on this one, Raney," and I will turn and catch a wave—I love these moments. Carmel, California. 2013. *Jeff Hawe*

Walking on the beach as a family in Baja, Mexico. One year we used this shot as our Christmas card. Todos Santos, 2017. *Rick Kessler*